Flights
Against the
Sunset

STORIES THAT REUNITED
A MOTHER AND SON

Flights
Against the
Sunset

Kenn Kaufman

Houghton Mifflin Company

BOSTON   NEW YORK

2008

For information about permission to reproduce selections from
this book, write to Permissions, Houghton Mifflin Company,
215 Park Avenue South, New York, New York 10003.

www.houghtonmifflinbooks.com.

Library of Congress Cataloging-in-Publication Data

Kaufman, Kenn.
  Flights against the sunset / Kenn Kaufman.
     p. cm.
  ISBN-13: 978-0-618-94270-1
  ISBN-10: 0-618-94270-x
  1. Bird watching — Anecdotes.   2. Bird Watchers —
Anecdotes.   3. Mothers and sons — Anecdotes. I. Title.
  QL677.5.K38 2008
  598.072'34 — dc22   2007041932

Book design by Anne Chalmers
Typefaces: Scala, Fairplex Wide

Printed in the United States of America

MP 10 9 8 7 6 5 4 3 2 1

TO MY EXTENDED FAMILY

or in other words,

to the Kaufman, Bader, Luzader,

Frey, Lortz, and Angelback families,

who showed me the essence of family:

crazy and beautiful, painful and glorious,

like life itself.

CONTENTS

A Note from the Author

Although this book is a memoir, the astute reader might suspect that a few episodes (such as the encounters with biker gangs and secret agents) may not have occurred exactly as described here. I include such episodes without apology, out of respect for my mother, who always taught us that the life of the imagination is as valid and as valuable as the life of the everyday.

ACKNOWLEDGMENTS

About two-thirds of the chapters included here first appeared, in different form and often under different titles, in the bimonthly *Bird Watcher's Digest* between 1988 and 2006, and I am grateful for permission to adapt that material for this book. My particular thanks to BWD founders Bill and Elsa Thompson, editor Bill Thompson III, and former editors Mary Beacom Bowers and Deborah Griffith, all of whom helped to shape some of the original stories.

In turning an eclectic collection of pieces into a cohesive story, I benefited greatly from the counsel of my agent, Wendy Strothman, who loves birds as well as books. Lisa White, at Houghton Mifflin Company, is one of today's foremost editors of natural history works, and she made major improvements to this book, as she has for all of my books in the last dozen years. Others at Houghton Mifflin who helped in various ways included Shelley Berg, Susan Brown, Gail Cohen, Martha Kennedy, Gretchen Needham, Clare O'Keeffe, and Taryn Roeder.

Finally, writing such an intensely personal story was difficult in many ways. I would not have attempted it without the encouragement and support of my lovely wife, Kimberly Kaufman, the brightest star in my heaven.

Flights
Against the Sunset
Sunset

"I FELT THE SAME WAY," JB told me. "It's awkward to talk about your trip halfway around the world when you know that she hasn't even been out in the hall for three months. But you know, she genuinely wants to hear it. All of it."

My brother had just come back from a film-history conference in Europe. I had just come back from leading a group on a nature tour in South America. Down the corridor from where we stood, our mother, going nowhere except gradually downhill, was lying in bed in a square white room on the fourth floor of a care and rehabilitation facility in Wichita, Kansas.

I had just arrived in town. At the conclusion of my South American tour, I'd gone home just long enough to clean up from the trip, and then I'd flown here, rented a car, and come straight to the rehab center, just as I always did. It had been six weeks since my last visit, and I was lingering in the hall, talking to JB, who was just leaving, while I steeled my nerves for the emotion of seeing her. Mom loved all four of her sons and she had never played favorites, but my three brothers all lived here in Wichita and they came in multiple times every week. I was the one who lived a thousand miles away. When I came here it was a different kind of visit.

In just a moment I would go on into the room. She knew I was coming, we made a point of not taking her by surprise, so I knew how it would go. She would be sitting up as best she could, and smiling, putting on a brave face, still determined to take care of her sons in any way she could manage, even if it were only to hide the pain and pretend that she was feeling fine. I would smile, too, and try not to show my shock at the fact that she would look even thinner than last time, the lines of pain etched deeper into her face. We would both put on this pretense for all the best reasons as I walked into the room.

Someone, either a staff person or one of my sisters-in-law, had washed her hair and put a ribbon in it. "Hello, beautiful," I said, kneeling next to the bed and hugging her as well as I could. "Your hair looks nice." I kissed her on the forehead.

"Oh, you," she said, the words slow and a little slurred. "Don't you know...it's not nice to lie to your mother."

"Oh, of course!" I said. "I would never do that!"

She had been beautiful all her life, but my father had loved her for her character and spirit, not just her looks. My father had adored her until the night he died, a night that had arrived with ferocious abruptness just a couple of years before. Married at twenty, never on her own, my mother had struggled with the agony and sheer terror of being alone for almost a year, and then a stroke had nearly taken her away. She had been in a coma for three weeks while my brothers and I stood vigil at the intensive care unit, deflecting the polite inquiries from doctors about pulling the plug, and then she had opened her eyes and started to come back to us. Mentally she came almost all the way back, and in a couple of months it was obvious that she knew us, she knew everything, and only her body was wasted and half paralyzed. Her speech was pained and slow, but she still knew all the words and she would bravely struggle to make conversation with anyone who came to visit.

I had begun making regular visits to Wichita, every few weeks, to do what I could to be helpful. There were still things to be done at the house — the house that we had moved into when I was nine, the house where Mom had lived with Dad for more than thirty years — and I wanted to do my part to help out. We were all operating on the stated belief that Mom's recovery would continue, that she would get better and better, and eventually she would be able to go home again, so we kept up all the standard maintenance, down to the level of mowing the lawn and cleaning the windows and even filling the bird feeder. So I would come to town with the idea of working around that house, but first I would go to see Mom, and she would beg me to stay and talk. And I would. I would sit by her bed and we would talk about everything, everything I could possibly think of to keep the conversation going, to keep her mind off of the pain. We would talk for three days, and then she would fight back the tears when I left for the airport to fly back home.

"So," I said, perching on the edge of a chair. "Are you causing plenty of trouble?"

"I'm trying," she said. "Doing my best."

"Keeping the staff awake at night with wild parties? Loud music, dancing girls? Although, I guess, dancing boys would be more like it."

"Dancing bears," she said. "I'm holding out for dancing bears."

"Good idea," I observed. "Doesn't take as many of them to make an impression."

"They...not easy to get," Mom said. Her speech was slow and halting, but she would persevere to finish a complete thought and to be understood. "I could probably call and get a pizza delivered. But nobody will deliver dancing bears."

"Well, here's an idea. Here's a way to combine two needs. We could start a pizza company that delivers, but instead of having pimply-faced teenagers bring the pizza, we could have it delivered by dancing bears. All we have to do is find the dancing bears and teach them to drive."

Mom gave me a long, doubtful look. "I guess it's a business model that has never been tried. Maybe for good reason."

"I can see it now. Bearly Edible Pizza, Incorporated. Do you want to be CEO?"

"If you got too close to the bears," she said, "it would be C E Owww."

We had always done this, she and my brothers and I, and sometimes my dad as well, we had always engaged in this kind of banter and wordplay. Mom's mind was still good enough for her to dream up interesting ideas and bad puns, and it was only physical strength that was lacking, making it hard for her to talk. But the strength of spirit was still there. She would act cheerful and as if everything was fine, hiding the discomfort that we knew she was feeling.

"Was it Africa this time?" she asked. "No . . . no, you were in South America, weren't you?"

"That's right," I said. "Northern South America. Venezuela again. I've been there a bunch of times now. I'll never know it like the U.S. or Mexico, but I feel like I'm starting to get a handle on the birds there."

"Tell me about your trip," she said. "I want to hear . . . all about it."

I paused before answering, and in that moment it occurred to me that I always had to pause, shift gears mentally, get myself into a different frame of mind before I started to tell her about my travels. It was always a challenge to describe my experiences to her, or to describe them to most of the people I met.

My lifelong passion for observing birds and nature had been a gift, a treasure, coming out of nowhere in earliest childhood. It had provided me an intensity of experience beyond what most people have in their daily lives. But it also had made it harder for me to communicate with those who did not share this level of fascination. If I told everything the way it truly happened, the way it felt, it would sound like an exaggeration to anyone who had not been there. So I often found myself applying a kind of conversion factor, toning everything down to a milder and more general description.

How could I describe my trip to South America in a way that would mean something to my mother? She already knew the basics: I was paid to act as a tour guide, leading groups of bird watchers to exotic destinations to show them types of birds that they had never seen before. It would be simple enough to say that our group had visited two main sites in the coastal cordillera and then had gone out to the flat llanos, the central plains of Venezuela. It would be simple enough to say that we had sixteen participants in the group and two of us leading the tour, simple enough to talk about the minibus and the hotels and the meals and the weather. But none of that would touch the essence, the core of the journey.

How could I describe the richness of the experience? I might want to tell my mother about the extraordinary variety of bird life in the tropics. For example, that the single nation of Venezuela, smaller than the state of Alaska, has twice as many different kinds of birds as all of the United States and Canada combined. But that comparison would mean something only to a person who had some concept of the bird life of the United States and Canada to begin with. To anyone else, it would be abstract in the extreme, the difference between x and two times x. I might try to fall back on numbers: to say that more than four hundred species of birds had been recorded here in the state of Kansas but that you'd have to bust a gut to see two hundred of those in a week during the peak of spring migration, while Venezuela hosts more than fourteen hundred species of birds and we might see over four hundred of those in a ten-day trip, despite the greater logistical challenges. But any such spewing out of raw numbers would turn off the most devoted listener. I dared not go that route.

How could I make the essence of the experience come alive? I had already encountered the difficulty of explaining the terms "bird watching" and "birding," which overlap in meaning and are both misleading. So many people —not my mother, she was tolerant of any approach, but other people—had expressed condescending amusement: "How can you just sit there and *watch* a bird?" As if it were some kind of toothless voyeurism. So many times I had tried to explain that it was mostly not a matter of watching, more an activity of seeking and finding and recognizing. That there was a sense of accomplishment in learning these birds: being able to go out to the tidal flats and recognize all the sandpipers, for example, to know the subtle differences among twenty species there. That on every trip afield we birders would find dozens of species of birds, most of them expected, a few not. That there was reassurance in going out and finding the wrens, flickers, kestrels, thrushes, finches right where we anticipated they would be. That there was reassurance in the expected seasonal patterns: the blackburnian warblers coming north on their way to Canada in April, the golden-plovers passing through southbound in September, the tree sparrows arriving for the winter in November, just as they did every year.

Then I might explain that the reassuring predictability of bird life was only half of the attraction — the other half was provided by the element of unpredictability, the chance for novelty. Birds have wings. Even on familiar ground there is always the chance that some totally unexpected bird will show up. And we could be sure that if we went to some new place, there would be new and different birds there. I had taken my tour group to Venezuela with full certainty that I would show them types of birds they had never seen before, but with no way to predict exactly which birds those would be. Birding is like a treasure hunt, with thousands of potential treasures waiting to be found.

How could I describe the heart of the experience? I might want to focus on one moment in the field, on a moment of learning, when my understanding increased and with it my three-dimensional view of my world. I might describe, for example, watching a mixed flock of birds moving through the treetops in the jungle at Rancho Grande. Looking out from the trail toward the steep downhill side, so that the tops of the nearby trees were at eye level, with sunlight filtering through and sparkling on drops of mist on the moss and bromeliads that covered the high branches. Focusing on a small brown bird called a streaked xenops and seeing, for the first time, how it would hammer on a branch with its little wedge-shaped bill, prying off a bit of dead bark to look for insects underneath, so that it was searching for food in a slightly different way than any of the twenty other kinds of birds traveling with it. One more tiny bit of information to add to my store of knowledge. But it was so hard to tell this in a way that would mean anything to a person who had not been there. My mother would listen if I told her, and she would try to care about the fact that I had learned something, but she could hardly be expected to care about the streaked xenops, a bird she had never heard of before and would never hear of again.

No, the truth was that I could not hope to communicate by talking about the birds themselves. For most of the people with whom I would be speaking, that was psychologically foreign territory, more distant and unfamiliar than the wilds of Venezuela. But I had to say something now. My mother was looking at me, waiting, her eyes shining as they always did when she looked at one of her sons — maybe shining also with a trace of tears, from trying to ignore the physical pain she was undoubtedly feeling. I had to tell her a story that would occupy her attention.

This was no time for dry details of ornithology. My subject matter would have to come from that frontier where the world of birds intersects with the world of the humans who pursue them.

THE GHOST
IN THE STATION

TWELVE MILES INLAND from the northern rim of
South America, two-thirds of a mile above the level of the
sea, the monstrous old building of Rancho Grande stares
back vacantly into history.

Its location is not the least of its mysteries. The site
was chosen by Juan Vicente Gómez, the last dictator of
Venezuela. Why he picked a steep jungle hillside in the
coastal range for the construction of a huge, gloomy,
three-story stone mansion, no one knew. When the dictator's death ended his reign in 1935, the workmen dropped
their tools and walked away, leaving the massive building
not quite completed. No one wanted to finish the job.

But the more enlightened government that followed
had a better idea. They designated a huge tract around it
as a national park and put the unfinished building of Rancho Grande to use as a biological field station. Naturalists
came here from many parts of the world, taking advantage of this convenient place to experience the rich diversity of the tropics. Most notable among these naturalists
was the great William Beebe, who spent several field

seasons at Rancho Grande, studying the diverse and abundant nature that was right outside the door.

Outside the door — or inside: because the station was not sealed off from the surrounding forest. Many of the windows had no glass, many of the doorways had no doors, and many of the forest creatures had no qualms about entering. Lizards climbed the walls, bats roosted in empty rooms, and swallows and swifts moved into the drainpipes. In dry weather, dead leaves drifted down the halls, while in rain a dozen rivulets ran through the building. The biologists made some improvements in the rooms they were using for their field laboratory and left the rest of the huge building to nature.

By the waning years of the twentieth century, the use of Rancho Grande had declined, and so had its condition. But here the members of the Baird Bird Club from Reading, Pennsylvania, came to pay their respects to the old biological station and to look for birds around it. My friend Victor Emanuel and I were leading their group on a private tour of Venezuela. Even though I had been here many times before, I was excited to be back at Rancho Grande, sharing this magical place with another group of friends. And it *was* a magical place — there was a special feeling in the air, a feeling produced by the history of the station, the miles of jungle surrounding it, and the array of tropical birds that paraded through the small clearing just in front of the building.

The birders from Reading, most of them on their first

visits to South America, were having the time of their lives. My friend Victor, enthusiastic as always, was up ahead pointing things out in all directions. There were more different kinds of birds here than one could ever hope to find at one spot in Pennsylvania: colorful tanagers of half a dozen sorts, several types of hummingbirds, a little gang of toucanets, a flock of parakeets streaking through the treetops. Overhead, a white hawk circled. In the thickets, a nightingale wren sang. And from the jungle behind the station, haunting and pervasive, came the ghostly whistles of the plain-backed antpitta.

I pointed out the voice of the antpitta for the group, and we all paused to listen. A series of low whistles on one pitch, it swelled in volume and then died away after about six notes, as if it had grown out of silence and then returned to silence. It was an appropriate voice for a wraith, for a phantom of the forest, or perhaps for an invisible bird.

This was mood music, I told the group, and nothing more. We had not a ghost of a chance of actually seeing the bird. Like most other antpittas, this one was a shy denizen of the forest floor, often heard but rarely seen. Round-bodied, short-tailed, long-legged, shaped like a grapefruit on stilts, it hopped and ran along the ground in the deepest and darkest parts of the jungle. Colored in muted browns, it would blend with the leaf litter even if it came out in plain sight, which it would never do. Imitations or recordings might bring it closer, but not too close. The plain-backed antpitta was astonishingly good at staying just out of sight.

So we appreciated it as a spirit voice while we watched the birds we could see. Toward midday, bird activity dropped off, and ours did, too; the group straggled back down the entrance road from the station toward the gate, where we had left the minibus.

Trailing behind, I stopped and looked back at the station. I loved this old building — but I could not quite explain why. After all, it was just a man-made structure. To a bird watcher it should have meant far less than the jungle around it. But in a way, perhaps because it had been here so long, it almost seemed as if it were a part of the jungle. I imagined the ghost of the great William Beebe coming back here for a visit; his ghost would walk the forest trails, no doubt, but I felt sure he would also walk the corridors of Rancho Grande, dreaming of his bygone days here of discovery and wonder.

Back at the vehicle, we were fixing a picnic lunch when someone asked, "Where's Rudy?" and someone else answered, "He's doing his thing. You know Rudy."

They knew him, all right. An authority on organic gardening who was also an expert botanist and birder, Rudy Keller was admired by everyone in the group. Contemplative, intensely curious, quietly independent, he had no doubt wanted to stay behind to look around the grand old biological station by himself. We could picture him there now, gazing at the old building or at the forest behind it with a reverent expression. That was the other thing you noticed about Rudy: his spiritual look. He looked — well, he looked like Jesus. His face looked exactly like the painted portraits of Jesus Christ that you see in church hallways and in Sunday school picture books. The other Reading birders told me that he had caused a sensation once, unintentionally, by walking through the lobby of a hotel where a preachers' conference was being held. Rudy shrugged off such talk, but the impression persisted.

"Here's what will happen," I said. "Rudy will meet the ghost of William Beebe, and you know what they'll do? They'll shake hands, and sit down for a serious discussion." Everyone laughed, but the tone of their laughter suggested that they knew I was not entirely joking.

But half an hour later, when Rudy finally came striding down the path to rejoin us, we could see immediately that something had happened. His face — which, on normal occasions, would have looked merely reverent — was transformed. Now he looked as if he had seen a miracle.

He had.

"I saw the *antpitta*," he announced. "I *saw* the antpitta. It came within a few feet of me."

While we stared at him in astonishment, he told his story. After we had left, Rudy had gone exploring. The Rancho Grande building, long and narrow, separated the clearing from the forested hillside behind, and at one point there was an open hallway at ground level that led the few yards through the building to the back. Walking through this gap, Rudy had found himself in the shadows of the jungle, with the ghostly whistle of the antpitta echoing around him. He could not tell the direction, but it had seemed very near, so he had waited, whistling soft imitations; and suddenly the bird had materialized in front of him. It had seemed fearless. Bouncing over the forest floor, it had come even closer to Rudy's position. Then, as suddenly as it had appeared, it had melted into the shadows again.

Victor Emanuel was visibly excited (not an unusual condition for Victor) at this news. Although he had been all over the tropics and had seen several other kinds of antpittas, he had never seen the plain-backed. As for me, I had seen it only once, after a serious effort; every other time, it had remained a voice in the forest. We all agreed that we should try for this bird at the point where Rudy had seen it, even though our chance for success seemed remote.

So early afternoon found all of us in the damp, deep shadows at the back of Rancho Grande. No sunlight penetrated to where we stood: the lofty jungle trees seemed to meet and then tower above the wall of the station, high overhead. A rocky, muddy hillside, tangled with roots and vines and massive tree trunks, began immediately behind the building. We could hardly see ten feet up the hillside through the riot of vegetation. And surrounding us was the haunting, taunting whistle of the antpitta, coming from everywhere and nowhere, like a sound created in the inner ear or in the brain.

Hoping to lure the bird closer, I began playing back a recording of its song — softly, sparingly. Birds often will respond to recordings of themselves, apparently thinking that a rival has invaded their turf. But it's easy to overdo it with recordings, a mistake I wanted to avoid. I would play one series of those ghostly whistles and then wait at least half a minute, sometimes a full minute, before playing another. The antpitta was answering from somewhere nearby...but we could not agree on whether it was coming closer, or even on the direction of the source. Anxiously we stared into the shadowy undergrowth, and waited.

My friend Victor has many talents, but sitting still for long periods is not among them, and this waiting game clashed with his action-oriented nature. He badly wanted everyone in the group to see this elusive and wonderful bird. Finally he whispered, "I'm going to go up the hill to see if I can get above this bird, to nudge it down in your direction." And he was gone, clambering catlike up the hillside, vanishing from sight almost immediately.

And we continued to wait. The stillness of the jungle closed in. Nothing moved on the thicket-choked hillside above us. We could not tell where Victor was. We could not tell where the antpitta was, either, but its voice still throbbed like fever in the brain.

Just when it seemed hopeless — when it seemed we

might never see even Victor again, let alone the antpitta — Rudy emerged from the shadowy opening in the building behind us. He had slipped away a few minutes earlier, and most of us had not noticed his departure. But we noticed his return. When we saw the expression on his face, we all stared.

Did I say earlier that Rudy looked as if he had seen a miracle? Okay, well, now he looked as if he had seen a dozen miracles, performed by two-headed rabbits from outer space. His expression was a mix of joy, amazement, and outright hilarity.

"I just saw the antpitta again," said Rudy. "It's behind you." Instinctively we turned to look, but nothing was there except the gray walls of Rancho Grande. "No, it's *in there*. The antpitta is *inside the building*."

While we gaped in disbelief, he told us what had happened. Rudy had waited with us for several minutes, and then it had occurred to him that he had already seen the bird as well as he was likely to, so he had gone exploring the inside of the station. And as he had walked the long, curving hallway — with the spectral whistle of the antpitta echoing around his ears as loudly as it had outside — a small form had materialized in the shadows ahead of him. It was a rotund, long-legged bird, hopping along the floor of concrete as it would have on the forest floor.

If you know bird watchers, you already know what happened next. It was a controlled dash: everyone hurried to get inside, but everyone waited to help others over the rubble piled in the doorway, and everyone did their best to keep quiet and to make sure that everyone else had a clear view down the hallway where Rudy was pointing.

From where we stood, the long corridor curved away gradually to the left. Along the right side were doorways leading to empty rooms, with windows that let in daylight from the clearing out in front. It was no darker for us inside the building than it had been in the jungle shadows behind it. And down the hall, silhouetted against an open doorway, was an unmistakable bird shape: big head squashed onto round body, with no neck and no tail; long, strong legs and big feet, seeming out of proportion to the bird they supported. Then the bird began to move, bouncing down the corridor with springy, big jumps, and everyone stared in amazement at the antpitta in action.

Everyone, of course, except Victor, who was still far up the hillside.

I went back out behind the building. The bird would be preoccupied with the group, I reasoned, and the walls would muffle the sound, so I could yell for Victor. And I had to: he was missing a bird he had never seen, just because he was trying so hard to find it for the group. "Victor!" I yelled. "Come on down! We've got the bird inside the building!"

The response was silence. Then, in a hushed voice — almost a stage whisper — from up the hill, Victor called back, "All right! I'm coming down! I'll circle around so I won't scare it away!"

He obviously didn't understand. I tried again. "No, just hurry down here! You won't scare it! It's inside the station!"

Victor told me later that he had heard me perfectly, but it had sounded so bizarre that he had refused to believe his ears. It seemed like hours (it must have been minutes, anyway) before Victor finally appeared, and we hurried into the building, down the long corridor to where the group was clustered.

During our absence, the antpitta had been quite cooperative. It had moved down the hallway, hopping and trotting through the shadows at a sedate pace, never quite outdistancing the group. At one point it had detoured into a side room—one that faced toward the clearing, the sunny side, but two of the birders had gone around the outside, peered in the window, and thus herded the bird back into the corridor. By the time we joined the group, the antpitta had moved all the way down to the end of the hall.

All the way. In fact, we did not even see it at first. "Is it gone?" I asked.

"Not quite," someone said. "You can see a sliver of it. Look at the base of the right-hand wall."

We looked. Beyond the doorless doorway was the glare of a sunny patch, dividing the shadow of the corridor from the endless shadows of the forest. That open, sunlit space would be a slight mental barrier: a deep-forest bird like the plain-backed antpitta would hesitate to cross it.

Reaching the end of the hallway, the antpitta had evidently edged around the corner in the shade; all we could see of it was a fraction of one wing.

For a moment we were perplexed. The bird was there, but we were not really seeing it. Any movement or noise we made might be enough to scare it away . . . and we would certainly never see it again once it regained the forest. What to do?

My hand moved toward the tape recorder—and stopped. Somehow, the tape seemed like the wrong answer. In my best whistle, my best low-pitched, soft, tantalizing whistle, I tried my own imitation of the antpitta's call.

And it worked. The bird suddenly turned around, so that we were seeing a different sliver of its body, but now its head was poking out, too, as it peered at us. Then out of the hidden shadows hopped the antpitta, to stand in full view for a long moment. Next to me, Victor was saying "Wowwwww" in a drawn-out, reverent whisper, and I could sense that everyone else had their binoculars raised again for another, final look at the antpitta. The bird bounced once on its long legs, and in a quick burst of flight it crossed the patch of sun to the safety of the forest.

Several minutes later we were all walking back down the entrance drive away from Rancho Grande, exulting over our fabulous fortune, when the sound began again: low and haunting, almost inaudible, without form or distance or direction, the call of the plain-backed antpitta. Was it behind the station, or back inside? We decided it didn't really matter. Spirits of the great naturalists would roam the halls of Rancho Grande as well as the trails outside, and so would the antpitta, seeming to know that one day the old building was going to be reclaimed by the forest.

MY MOTHER WAS LOOKING at me with her eyes open wide, and I could tell she was making an effort to concentrate, to be sure she didn't miss anything. "I'm so proud of you," she said. "Your groups always want to see rare birds...and you're so good at showing them. Everything."

"Thanks," I mumbled. "Actually I didn't show them this antpitta thing. Rudy found it, twice, and we all just got to see it. Happens that way a lot on these trips — the people in the group find a lot of the birds."

"But you still take the people where they can see these birds. And you told them what this...antpitta?...was before they saw it."

"Yeah, I'm like the facilitator. I'm not the bank robber, I just drive the getaway car. No, seriously, I enjoy the work. It's not research — although I might do some of that before the group arrives or after they go home. It's not exactly education. I try to teach people things, but mostly they come on the trips to have a good time. So it's really a kind of entertainment, and I try to wrap up some inspiration and education in it. But you can't orchestrate the trip in any detail because the birds are so unpredictable. Mostly you just have to stay flexible and take advantage of whatever opportunities come up."

"I'm not very flexible these days," Mom said, grimacing a little as she shifted in bed. "I wouldn't make a very good bird watcher." There was a long, awkward moment of silence while I tried to think of something positive to say. Then she looked back at me. "What was the rare bird that you found last year in Alaska? It was something... something like a curfew. But that wasn't it."

"You're right," I said, a little too enthusiastically, realizing as I said it that my brothers and I kept on doing this: we were so eager to grasp every instance of Mom remembering details about things or processing information well, eager to tell ourselves that her mind was still sharp and that she was getting better. "Yes, you're right, almost the same thing. The bird was called a curlew."

"That place where you saw it," she said, "I can never remember what it's called. You'd been there before. Some ... some Eskimo village. But not with an Eskimo name."

So she really was remembering. Mentally I kicked myself for having doubts. She wanted me to tell her that story again, so I did.

CURLEW AFTER CURFEW

I NEED TO START by describing the place to you, and there are two basic things you need to know about it: location and weather. The Eskimo village of Gambell has a deceptively gringoized name, but it's located far out in the vast, cold wilderness of the Bering Sea, closer to Asia than to the mainland of Alaska. Gambell is at the northwestern tip of long, narrow St. Lawrence Island, and at times of clear weather you can stand in the village and see the cliffs of Siberia all along the northwestern horizon. More often, though, you can stand in Gambell and not even see Sevuokuk Mountain, barely a mile away to the east. The fog may not lift until it is chased out by sleet or rain or snow (or all three), driven by winds born at the North Pole. The weather here can change rapidly, and it often does, usually for the worse.

These conditions make Gambell an uncertain place for things that fly. In a way, that was why I had brought my group here. And in a way, that was why my friend Gary was still here, two days after he had planned to leave.

I was leading a group on a bird-watching tour of Alaska, and we had come to Gambell partly to look for birds that didn't belong in Alaska at all. The position of St. Lawrence Island, and the patterns of weather around it, mean that birds migrating north on the Asian side of the Bering Strait can easily get confused or blown off course and end up here. Our tour group was hoping to find some such Siberian strays. On the day that we arrived at Gambell, another birding group was leaving — at least, most of them left. The sturdy but small planes of the local airline, Bering Air, could carry only so much at a time. One person had to be left behind. Gary Rosenberg, one of the leaders of the other group (and an old friend of mine from Arizona birding days), was elected to stay on the island one more night — he would fly out on the first plane the next morning.

Except that there was no plane the next morning. The fog had rolled in by then.

Gambell can be a magic land for birders. I had fallen in love with the place when I had come here alone at the age of nineteen. Lying just below the Arctic Circle, Gambell has almost enough light in early summer for birding around the clock: the sun sets at 1:30 in the morning, and comes up again a couple of hours later. And plenty of birds are there to fill the hours of daylight.

Most of the types present are seabirds or water birds of northern affinities. Various members of the auk family, such as auklets and murres, nested on the island's cliffs by the thousands, while puffins and the small gulls called kittiwakes were here by the hundreds. Several kinds of loons and big eider ducks would fly past the northwest point of the island every evening, along with flocks of the rare emperor goose. And when it came to land birds, no assumptions from the mainland applied here. That little bird hopping around in the village would never be a mere house sparrow: it was at least some northern specialty like a redpoll or white wagtail, maybe a bluethroat, maybe even some rare wanderer from Siberia like a reed bunting or a rosefinch.

Still, we could hardly blame Gary for being ready to leave. He had had well over a week of trudging through snow and gravel. He had spent dozens of hours freezing on the shore at the northwest point, watching the seabird passage. He had made dozens of walks through the "boneyards," areas that had been whale-carcass dumps for the Eskimos in centuries past and that were now the best land bird habitats around Gambell. Now he was ready to have a hot shower, sleep in a bed, walk on firm ground, write up his bird notes in comfort.

I had been the only birder on the island during my visit as a teenager, but I was far from alone now. Our tour group — about a dozen participants plus Kevin Zimmer, Dave Sonneborn, and me — had rented a house for our stay in Gambell. Sharing our quarters were Paul Lehman and Gary Rosenberg, who had come out as leaders of another tour group and were staying on with us: Paul intentionally, Gary unintentionally. A Four Points birding tour group had rented a house on the far side of the village, and an informal group from Houston had yet another spot. Early June birding at Gambell had become popular.

With so many birders on the island, the watchword was cooperation, not competition. All the group leaders carried radios, and we would check in every half hour to share information on sightings. News traveled fast. When it became obvious that Gary was going to be stranded a second unplanned night, that news made the rounds with the bird reports.

Everyone reacted to Gary's plight as you would expect friends to react: by razzing him unmercifully. "Seen any planes recently, Gary?" "Did your group bribe Bering Air *not* to come back for you?" "We'll bring you a clean shirt when we come next year." Gary was good-natured enough to go along with the joke, and he began referring to Gambell as "The Land That Bering Air Forgot," in stentorian tones, like a movie title. But we could see that the local magic was wearing thin on him.

Gary's third day of exile began with cold wind and a dense, low cloud cover, far too low for any plane to land. But this is the kind of weather that produces sightings of lost birds. The Houston group found a terek sandpiper, an odd little Asian shorebird with an upturned bill, at the far boneyards, and our whole group trekked out to see it. Then someone else found a rustic bunting nearby, and we all looked at that. This was a fine double shot of uncommon strays from the Asian side of the Bering Sea, and Gary enjoyed these birds as much as anyone, even though he had seen both species in Alaska before. But by afternoon he was getting depressed.

"I talked to the agent for Bering Air," he told me. "He says the visibility is still too poor. The plane won't come from Nome until the guy here gives the go-ahead, and he won't unless he's really sure. And you know how it sometimes clears up in the evening? That's no help — the pilots can only fly within a set number of hours after they start in the morning. I may be stuck here another night. I can't believe my luck."

"Gary," I said, "bad plane weather is good bird weather. Maybe some fabulous bird will show up this afternoon."

"I'm not holding my breath waiting for it," he said. "I'm under a curse. This is The Land That Bering Air Forgot."

No fabulous birds showed up that afternoon. Nice ones, yes, but not fabulous. A red-throated pipit at the foot of the mountain performed for us, doing flight songs against the gray sky, and a small sandpiper called a red-necked stint showed up near the airstrip. After dinner we had great studies of an ivory gull along the beach. None of these birds was outlandish by Gambell standards, but they helped add up to a satisfying day for those of us who had expected to be here.

Late that evening Kevin, Dave, and I were sitting out at the northwest point, watching the flights of auklets over the tiderips offshore, and our conversation drifted to the topic of rare birds. For a while we swapped stories of rarities we had sought and seen. We all agreed on one point: there is nothing like being there at the initial discovery. Going to see someone else's find can be fun, but it can't compare to that moment of discovery — that heart-pounding, short-of-breath realization that this bird is something completely unexpected. Such moments are rare in the lives of most birders, but the mere hope for them adds spice to many an hour in the field.

At eleven-thirty that night we made the usual half-hour check on the radio, but no one answered except Gary and Paul. They were heading back to the house. We decided to do the same. There would be enough light for at least two more hours of birding, but it had already been a long day, and we were sure that the day's excitement was over.

Trudging back through the gravel, I was lost in thought, not really paying attention. But Dave looks for birds all the time, even in his sleep, and he was looking now. "Shorebird coming over," he called out. We stopped to look up at the lone bird passing overhead.

Shorebirds — the collective term for the sandpipers, plovers, and their relatives — have a special fascination for avid birders. There are dozens of different kinds, all with trim, elegant shapes and beautiful, understated plumage patterns. Many of them are strong fliers and long-distance migrants, nesting in the high Arctic and spending their winters on the southern continents. Their powers of flight are so impressive that if they go off course, they may go extremely off course. A sandpiper that nests in Arctic Canada and typically winters in southern South America might make a mistake and wind up in southern Africa instead, or Australia. But the serious birder looks at shorebirds mainly for the challenge of telling the species apart, and for the beauty of these subtle birds.

After you've spent time looking at shorebirds, you come to the point where you can recognize most of them on the wing. Each type has its own distinctive shape and flight style. After so many thousand hours of haunting the mud flats, you can call them in the air: stolid dowitchers, quick darting solitaries, slim yellowlegs, chunky knots, elongated godwits, and all the rest. I had done my time; so when Dave announced the passing shorebird, I looked up with the full expectation that it would look familiar.

But it didn't.

Trim and medium-sized and fast like a golden-plover, but it wasn't shaped like a plover. Head and neck like those of an upland sandpiper, but its bill was too long, its tail too short. Overall shape and color like those of a tiny godwit or curlew, but it looked far smaller than even a whimbrel, and its bill seemed to be straight. It was all wrong. In that first split second my mind scrambled for logic, for firm footing, and I felt an electric tingling of the sort that mountaineers feel just before lightning strikes. Why, in all the world there were only two shorebirds known that looked like this. One was probably extinct, and had cinnamon underwings, which this bird lacked. And the other one . . .

"I think it's a little curlew," I said.

Kevin lowered his binoculars and stared at me. He knows that I seldom make snap calls on poorly seen birds. Now he seemed to be wondering if I had lost my mind.

I was wondering the same thing.

The little curlew is no everyday shorebird. It is found strictly in the Old World, and it is not common there: it nests on remote central Soviet grasslands, wintering largely in the Australian outback and stopping over at few points in between.

Only one little curlew had ever been documented in the New World. It had been found, coincidentally, by our friend Paul Lehman, the same guy who was now sharing the Gambell house with us. That bird had stayed for four weeks in the fall of 1984, in fields of southern California. Four years later, there had been a tantalizingly brief sighting in the same area. But there had not been a trace of a little curlew in Alaska, or anywhere else in the great gap between southern California and central Asia.

Adding to the aura of the little curlew is the fact that it is the closest relative of the legendary Eskimo curlew — a bird from America's past, a bird somewhere out on the hazy edge of extinction.

All of this went through my mind in a lot less time

than it takes to describe it. Meanwhile, the enigmatic shorebird had dwindled to a speck over the Bering Sea, but then — "It's coming back," called Dave. "The bird is coming back." And it was, arrowing in toward us, seeming to drop in just behind the next low ridge.

We hurried to the spot and saw — nothing. Nothing but gravel and snow. We went on over the next low ridge, and the next, and finally stood looking up and down the empty shoreline. The bird was nowhere in sight.

The three of us looked at one another in consternation.

Dave, who loves rare birds anyway, was already favoring the idea of little curlew: a first for Alaska. But I could see Kevin's mind working furiously, as the scientist in him strove to reject my initial call. "It did look a little like a miniature curlew," he said. "But the bill looked *straight*. Maybe it was a ruff."

"Not a ruff," said Dave. "No white on the rump. I could see that when it turned."

"Or maybe an upland sandpiper?"

"Not an upland sandpiper," I said. "The shape was wrong. Really — I haven't seen all the shorebirds in the world, but I've studied up on them — nothing else fits. I couldn't see any cinnamon color under the wings, so I don't think it's an Eskimo curlew. It has to be a little curlew."

But a minute later, on the radio, my conviction began to falter. No one answered the call except Paul and Gary, back at the house now. "You only saw the bird in flight?"

"Well...yeah. I know it sounds crazy, but I, um, can't think of what else it might have been."

Paul's long silence spoke volumes. Finally, "Tell you what. Why don't you give us another call if you find the bird on the ground? We'll leave the radio on here."

I stuffed my radio back in my coat pocket and looked up blankly at the sky. *It had to be a little curlew*, I said to myself. Again I imagined that swift form hurtling overhead, sweeping wide over the ocean, seeming to come back to us, and then vanishing. *It had to be. But where could it be now?* In the vast wilderness of the Arctic, little curlews had been found nowhere within a thousand miles of here — nowhere in Alaska, nowhere in far eastern Siberia. Maybe this bird knew in some way that it was really lost, beyond any hope of return; maybe it was going to keep flying into the frozen North, flying into oblivion, mindless of the crazy coincidence that it had flown past three birders who suspected what it was. I felt an ache inside. This little curlew might be lost to us just as the Eskimo curlew was lost: not gone, perhaps, but forever out of reach.

It was then that Kevin had his brilliant idea. Kevin is as much a scientist as a birder, and one of his strong points is an ability to analyze habitats, to predict where birds are going to be. Now he said, "Okay, listen to this. Suppose — just suppose — this bird really was a little curlew. Or suppose it was something like a ruff or an upland sandpiper. None of those birds would come down on a gravel beach — they like open fields. What's the closest thing we have to an open field? That big grassy area by the airstrip. I think we should look there."

It was about a twenty-minute walk up through the village to the airstrip. No one was around. The sled dogs dozed at the ends of their chains, and their modern counterparts, the snowmobiles and three-wheelers, were parked in silence. Even though it was still broad daylight, Gambell was asleep; after all, it was nearly midnight.

Kevin had reached the edge of the airstrip ahead of us. I saw him raise his binoculars to his eyes once, a casual motion, and then lower them again. He looked back at us impatiently.

"What a lazy bum," I grumbled. "Kevin isn't even willing to *look* for this bird until we get up there to help him."

"That may not be what's happening," said Dave. "Look at his face. Kevin has an awfully funny look on his face."

We were almost up to him now, and Kevin was indeed wearing a very odd expression. He looked like he had just been gored by a unicorn. "I was going to *wait* for you guys," he began, in a strangled tone, "but then I thought maybe I'd scan a little. Only I didn't scan. I just raised my binocs one time, and there it *was...*"

And there it was! A heart-stopping ten yards away, so close that it seemed any movement might frighten it, was the tiniest curlew we had ever seen. Patterned in soft browns, it blended perfectly into the tawny, dry grass. Its only markings of distinction were on its face, where a broad, buffy eyebrow was bordered above and below with black stripes. In shape it was a perfect miniature curlew, right down to that distinctive bill: thin, delicate, almost straight, barely down-curved. None of us had seen a little curlew before, but we all knew that we were seeing one now.

Alerted by radio, Paul and Gary made it to the airstrip in record time, with a couple of the more serious members of our tour group not far behind. The bird had not wandered far from its original spot. In a moment we were all looking at it. Paul doesn't show his emotions much, but we could tell he was reliving the excitement he had felt on finding the first little curlew for California. "That's what it is, all right," he said softly. Studying the bird intently, he began to list the field marks that made it a little curlew, not an extinct Eskimo curlew nor an undersized whimbrel or anything else.

Dave was enjoying all this immensely, but— "We need to rally the other birders!" he cried. Again he put out a call on the radio, but there was no answer. So he set off, with long strides, toward the house of the Four Points group. Seen through binoculars, his arrival brought to mind a ferret entering a prairie dog mound: Dave charged into the house, and a minute later birders came piling out in all directions, pulling on jackets and boots, heading for the airstrip.

Next, at the house where most of our tour group was

still trying to sleep, Dave arrived like a friendly hurricane. "Come on, you have to get up and come see this bird... no, you can't wait until morning; it might be gone then... yes, I'll show you a red-necked stint, too, if you come out ... but you have to come out now!" Dave's persuasive energy worked wonders, and a growing crowd collected on the grass by the airstrip to pay respects to the little curlew.

A few minutes later I noticed that Gary was grinning from ear to ear, like a Cheshire cat that has just eaten a dozen canaries. "I can't believe my *luck*!" he said. "If the flights had been on schedule, I would have *missed* this bird!"

"I guess Bering Air is Gary's favorite airline right now," Paul observed.

"Here, look at this," said Kevin. "How often do you get to see this at one-thirty in the morning?"

We all looked. The sky had miraculously cleared toward the north and west, casting the scene in a light that was soft but intense. A huddle of birders stood motionless, in an almost reverent silence behind their binoculars and scopes, while the only little curlew within a thousand miles fed unconcernedly a few yards away from them.

And it *was* one-thirty in the morning at Gambell. We had proof: beyond the American birders, beyond the distinguished Asian shorebird, beyond the waters of the Bering Sea, beyond the Siberian mountains that now glowed along the entire northwestern horizon, the sun was going down.

SHE SPOKE SLOWLY and with difficulty, but her eyes were shining, and it was something she wanted to say. "You tell the story so well," she said. "You should ignore what that teacher told you. No . . . what the teacher told JB. She said . . . If you want to know whether you have talent, don't ask your mother. But your mother knows about these things. I studied all this."

She had. Years before, she had studied all this: not my field of biology, not anything scientific, but many things artistic. I had heard her stories about her time in college, but frequently I would ask her to tell me again, at times when she was feeling strong enough to talk, because when she talked about those years, it took her away from present pain and back to what might have been the best time of her life. And I wanted to hear it. By listening to what she said, and listening more closely to the things she left unsaid, I could glean a portrait of her — not just as the person filling the role of "mom" but as an individual. Maybe it was disrespectful for a grown man to think of his own mother as a nineteen-year-old college student, but sometimes she thought of herself that way, and in a sense that was still at least a part of who she was.

She had grown up in the Midwest and had led a sheltered childhood, as sheltered as it could be during the Great Depression and then World War II. She had spent her first years living in small towns in Iowa and then in Oklahoma, with parents who were loving but strict. The possibilities had always seemed sharply limited. But then she had gone to the university, and suddenly the world had changed. Suddenly the possibilities had stretched out to the horizon. There was a whole universe of things to explore, the world of ideas and the world of art and history and philosophy. She had professors who knew the world, who had lived in Boston and London and Rome. She dreamed of going there herself, performing Shakespeare onstage in New York, discussing literature in the salons of Paris. For this young lady, at the age of nineteen, it seemed that anything was possible.

And then she had met a young man who had also seen something of the world. He had been in Europe, not for the dangerous and victorious part of the war but for the grim and messy task of the cleanup afterward, and he was looking for something clean, wholesome, and solid to help him forget what he had seen. The two of them, the young lady and this young man, got married and settled down and started a family. And for that young lady, the great wide world out there never got any closer than it had been when she was nineteen.

Some of this I read between the lines, reading my own interpretation into that brief, wistful pause before she went on, as she always did, to talk about the adventure of being married and raising a family. She had poured her heart into raising her four sons. If pressed, no doubt she would have said that she would do exactly the same thing again, that she loved the experience of her family and she would not have traded it for the world. In a sense, though, she had in fact traded the world for this. Or at least the potential for the world. She had passed up her chance at boundless possibilities and had passed them along to us.

She was never a guilt-trip mother. I have met a few of those parents who seem intent on instilling a sense of guilt in their children, and I've seen the lasting effects of that parental approach, and she was definitely not one of those. It took me years to figure out that she and my father had made major sacrifices for us. Once it had dawned on me, though, I felt that I owed her this: if she asked me to tell her about my experiences, I had an obligation to tell them just as true and as clear as I could.

EAGLE DREAMS

WE HAD BEEN given directions to the place where a pair of harpy eagles had built a nest near a trail in the extensive rainforest near the Guyana border. The information was many months old, and we were sure that the young eagle would have grown up and fledged and that the birds would be long gone. We knew, too, that this teeming region held hundreds and hundreds of other bird species that we could have sought, with much more chance of success. But we went there on a stubborn search for an eagle that would not be there, because this harpy eagle was a specific bird we knew about, one that we wanted to see.

The harpy eagle is a huge bird, the most formidable bird of prey in the world. It is a fittingly powerful creature to reign over the jungles centered on the Amazon, the world's mightiest river. This eagle feeds upon monkeys, sloths, great iguanas, and big birds like curassows and guans when they venture to the treetops, doing its hunting far above the ground but just below the leafy canopy of the forest. When the harpy eagle is on the hunt, it glides silently among the topmost branches of the trees.

When it soars above the forest, which may not happen very often, it may circle just above the treetops or it may rise so high as to go unseen by watchers on the ground. Like its jungle neighbor the jaguar, a harpy eagle is a magnificent predator of the green shadows, generally evading human eyes.

So we journeyed to the site of the reported nest, knowing that the birds would have moved on, knowing it was absurd to hope for an encounter, but hoping anyway.

On the narrow trail, my friends and I walked in single file, and in silence; the rainforest encourages you to be alone with your thoughts. My own dominant thought was that this was a complicated place. It was not complicated in color theme—everything in sight was some shade of green or brown—but this rainforest vegetation was a riot of complexity, layer upon layer of life.

Starting at the ground, there was underfoot the endless decay of the centuries of the forest. Fallen trunks and damp brown leaves were rotting into soil, nudged along by legions of fungi, the meager organic capital of the fallen vegetation to be devoured again by more growing things. Above them by a foot or two was the first layer of green: undergrowth plants that obviously thrived in the shadows, because rarely would any ray of direct sun filter down to this level. Next came scattered small trees, two or three times the height of a man, either more shadow dwellers or those striving upward to reach the light. There were bigger trees, with bigger trunks, most of their branches concentrated eighty feet or more above our heads, their crowns in the sun. Growing over all the branches were epiphytic plants: mosses, big, bulging bromeliads, and inconspicuous orchids. Vines grew here, too, scaling the trunks like thieves, their leaves swarming like pirates into any sunlit gap.

And here beside the trail was a really big tree, a grandfather tree, its trunk as wide as the five men at the base. From the broad, buttressed base, the trunk rose smooth and unbroken as a column of stone, with no branches at all within a hundred feet of the ground. Only where it drew level with the tops of the other trees did the massive limbs flare out in six directions, rising still higher to a leafy crown above the roof of the forest. Where the branches diverged at the top of the trunk, the edges of a mass of dead sticks revealed the location of the harpy eagles' nest. We stood around the base of the tree, heads tilted back, mouths open, staring up toward the nest in silence.

We were only transients here, visitors of a moment. But the harpy eagle, spending a lifetime in this place, would never have the view of the rainforest that we were having now. The eagle lived in the upper stories of the trees. In the natural order of things, it had no reason ever to come to the forest floor. It had no reason to come down to the level of man — not unless man brought it down.

Once, in the motley collection of a zoo in a Latin American town, I had seen a harpy eagle in a cage. Any eagle in a cage, robbed of freedom and flight, is only half a bird; but even this half was impressive enough: its legs as thick as my wrists, talons ending in curved claws more than an inch long, great feathery crest like a helmet on its head, massive hooked beak...broad shoulders, with drooping wings that would never fly again. What a magnificent bird this must have been, I thought, before it was caged. I wanted to see it in the wild, in its element.

So we stood on the dark forest floor, looking up in silence, squinting at the brightness of sky that sifted through the high leaves of the eagle tree. Waiting—without knowing quite what we waited for, since we knew the bird would not return. Still, we could almost imagine what it would be like.

This bird would be nothing like the bald eagles or golden eagles that we knew in North America, sitting aloof in the bare treetops to scan for rabbits or dead fish. This was a guerrilla eagle of the deep forest. With eyesight and hearing far more precise than ours, with an awareness of every movement and sound within a wide perimeter, the harpy eagle would know we were here. That big, double-pointed crest on its head would be raised, no doubt, as it looked down with a fierce gaze. Those massive shoulders would be hunched, the wings ready to open, the thick talons tensed, as it stood alert for any threat, ready to fly again and to disappear into the green wilderness.... But only if the bird were here, of course, and it was not. Birds were all around us, but not the harpy, not the one we wanted to see.

I have said that this forest was a complicated place. For me it was complicated in another important way: I was unprepared.

After several trips to northern and western Venezuela, I thought I knew the birds of those areas fairly well. But only a little farther south and east into South America, the bird life changed dramatically. Literally hundreds of new and different bird species appeared. We were in that zone of abundant novelty now. And I had had no time beforehand to prepare for the birds here.

Always in the past, before traveling to any exotic place, I had spent long hours studying every available bird book for that region. My aim had been to learn the characteristics of the local birds, so that I would recognize them when I saw them. But now I was realizing that this advance preparation accomplished something else. It gave each bird a kind of identity. It gave each bird a distinct character, and made each one more meaningful when it appeared.

On this trip, with no such preparation, new birds seemed to come out of nowhere: What's that? Must be slender-footed tyrannulet. Slender-footed? Yeah, there are so many tyrannulets, all looking the same, they ran out of good names for them. Okay, but, frankly, I've never heard of it. What's this? Looks like a spot-crowned woodcreeper, but that isn't found here, so it must be a lineated wood-creeper, assuming that *is* found here. Unless it's something else. Right. On and on they came, these antwrens, bristle-tyrants, spinetails, foliage-gleaners, euphonias, tree-hunters, flatbills, leaftossers, a blur of unfamiliar or half-remembered birds.

Never before had I realized how much my appreciation of birds was affected by prior knowledge. This point had dawned on me, gradually, only during the preceding few days. It came to me with more force as we stood looking up at the eagles' nest. An odd sensation came over me, too, as my mind drifted to scenes and settings very different from those around us now. Standing in the shadows of the tropical forest, surrounded by huge, name-less trees, bizarre insects, exotic tropical flowers, and the shrieks of unknown birds, I was taken by incongruous daydreams about other lands, a world away from here. I was thinking about Europe.

I was thinking of the country lane where I had seen my first European robin, and of the impact of seeing this little bird. In itself it was not an impressive creature — it was only half the size of the American robin. But this was the bird taken to heart by many centuries of Britons and Europeans. Given a familiar English name by the country people, it had in turn given its name to dozens of birds on continents that Western science discovered later: American robins, Australian robins, African robin-chats, Asian bush-robins, and all the rest. Any one of those namesakes might be more colorful, or more tuneful, but no matter. This little bird on the roadside was the *original* robin, the one I had heard about and read about for years, the one I had always wanted to see.

So it was with so many other European birds. Here was the European goldfinch, the original goldfinch, a bird that had figured in myths and legends since medieval times. Here was the sky lark, whose song had inspired poems by Keats and Shelley. Here were the black-headed gulls that Niko Tinbergen had watched, the geese that Peter Scott had painted, the greenshanks that Eric Hosking had photographed, the titmice that David Lack had studied. Here were birds known by the same colorful names given to them for generations: jackdaw, rook, chaffinch, fieldfare, brambling. Every new bird was one I already knew, in some way, through the recorded history of its importance to a tradition of naturalists.

Now in South America, in that region where the teeming tropical forests of the Amazon Basin blend northward toward the Orinoco Delta, there might have been more kinds of birds in a few square miles than exist in all of Europe — but they were anonymous birds. Most had never been studied; many had never been photographed or painted; none had ever inspired classic poetry. Most had English names coined by scientists sitting in dusty museums four thousand miles away. Most had never been heard of by anyone except those scientists. A prominent exception, of course, was the harpy eagle, a bird powerful enough and elusive enough to have sparked legends and desires.

That was why I held to this absurd hope and waited, watching the empty nest in the massive tree. And of course the harpy eagle never came. It might have been a mile away or a hundred miles away in the leafy wilderness of the treetops, and we never would have known. And finally my friends brought me back from reveries of the distant and the impossible to the steamy jungle of the present, where, they said, we were wasting time. The eagle would not appear, they said, and there were hundreds of other birds that we should be seeking.

So we went to seek those other birds. We found many of them, and we watched them and listened to them and wrote notes and made sketches and did everything we could to make those birds a part of our experience. And it worked, for a while. We got to feel as if we knew some of them fairly well.

But that was only until we went home to the States. Within a few weeks or months, despite our best intentions, the memories would begin to blur. Then we would have to struggle to remember anything about that little flycatcher or woodcreeper or antbird, whatever its name was, that we had seen in the forest.

But we would never forget the eagle we had not seen. In the jungles of our dreams the great bird would come in again, gliding through the maze of the highest branches, its head hunched back onto broad shoulders, huge wings starting to tilt and push back against the air, long tail spread wide to brake the glide, massive talons reaching and grasping, settling onto a limb, the big head turning with crest raised high as the eagle peered down through the shadows at the puny earthbound humans standing so far below...again, over and over, forever in the imagination.

As a kid I had never been a mama's boy by any stretch of the imagination. The things that fascinated me were almost all outdoors, and Mom was not much of an outdoors person, aside from a few desultory attempts at gardening. Dad had no particular knowledge of nature, but he did enjoy getting outside, and he would take the boys on camping trips, where I would run around like a little maniac looking for new birds or insects or reptiles or anything else in the way of natural history novelty. So I had more of a bond with my father than with my mother, but Dad didn't talk much, so when I was with him I didn't, either. I never talked to my parents very much about my obsession with birds while I was still living at home.

Of the many influences for which I could thank my parents, one of the biggest ones involved television — or, rather, lack of television. My parents didn't see much value in TV, and they didn't have one in the house. My brothers and I had to come up with other things to amuse ourselves. And we did. We all came up with strong interests, all different. Mom used to say that she lived in a house with a bachelor and four only sons. JB, the oldest, went from drawing cartoons to studying how animated cartoons and other films were made, then learned to play half a dozen musical instruments and wrote songs on all of them. I read history or classics of literature when the weather was extremely bad, but if it was possible to be outside, I was out there pursuing birds or other aspects of nature. My younger brother Rick was most like Dad: he could do everything, build anything, fix anything, and he got to the point where he probably could have taken a motorcycle apart and put it back together blindfolded. Ralph, the youngest, tried to emulate Rick, but he also had a strong literary streak, writing fiction and essays and poetry and song lyrics. When the four of us were together, the conversation could go in any direction. But for the most part, I didn't talk about birds that much. It was too hard to express my fascination with the natural world, so it became like a treasure I was hoarding for myself.

At school, likewise, I seldom said anything about natural history. One of my classmates, Jeff Cox, had picked up on my interest and had become just as rabid a birder as I was, but we didn't talk about birds during school hours. No, instead, we formed a gang. Coxie's Army, we called ourselves, just four guys who shared most of the same honors classes. We had all read Rudyard Kipling's *Stalky & Co.* and had been inspired by it. While idly wondering why a junior high school library would be so rash as to have such a troublemaking book on the shelves, we tried to match the exploits of Stalky and Beetle and McTurk in causing mayhem at school without actually getting in trouble ourselves. But when the closing bell rang, I was out the door, headed to the river or the woods or the sandpit ponds, focused on birds, everything about school forgotten. I led a double life then, and I rarely even tried to connect the two orbits in which I traveled.

The few times that I did try, I was served with powerful reminders of the fact that birding really was an alien concept for most of the people in the other half of my world.

Your Eyes Are Like Limpid Pools, Whatever That Means

BY THE TIME I reached the age of thirteen, I had been fascinated by birds for all of seven years, or more than half my life. They represented boundless mystery to me, and elusiveness, and beauty. But by the age of thirteen I had started to notice other things in nature as well, other things of beauty: Butterflies. Frogs. Beetles. Trees. Turtles. Ferns. Wildflowers. I was drawn to everything that symbolized what it meant to be intensely alive.

Every chance I had, every afternoon after school, I would go outdoors, looking for birds, trying to identify plants, catching insects or reptiles. But not this afternoon. This afternoon was special in a different way. I knew that my parents and my big brother would laugh if I dared to call it a "date," but it was something, anyway: Tamara, the prettiest girl in my English class, had agreed to meet me after school so we could ride our bikes down to the river.

This was a new kind of experience for me. I really had no idea how to talk to a girl. After all, I had no sisters. My father treated my mother like the queen of the world every day, and my brothers and I were raised to treat all women with the utmost respect. Of course, I knew plenty of girls at school, but I didn't know any of them well; to me, they were all distant and mysterious.

Girls were just so *different*. Consider Tamara, now. I was casting sidelong glances at her as we rode side by side: the way the loose strands of her red-blond hair curled against the side of her neck. The way she pushed the pedals, lightly, with the toes of her tennis shoes. The graceful angle of her wrists slanting down to the handlebars. She was *perfect*, that's all, the way a bluebird or a robin or an oriole was perfect when you got to see it up close. And I . . . I was just a gangly, awkward thirteen-year-old, lacking confidence, dimly sensing that Tamara was a lot older than I in some important ways. She could have been out with the older boys, the ones who were old enough to drive. Why was she here at all, anyway? Maybe it was a joke, and at any moment she would give a pretty laugh and then pedal away from me.

She didn't, though. We arrived together at my favorite spot by the river, where big willows lined the bank. The biggest willow stood back from the water's edge and leaned far over, so that the main trunk was almost horizontal, with limbs rising from it. You could sit there, surrounded by shady green, and look out through a window among the branches at the quiet flow of the river. I had sat there often by myself, watching to see if a solitary sandpiper would come tripping along the bank, or perhaps a family of goldfinches would flutter down for a drink. Today I had my binoculars along, of course, but they were hidden under the jacket in my bicycle basket, and I didn't think I should start by telling Tamara about the birds here.

The natural bench of the willow trunk was long enough that we could both sit there without being too close together, so Tamara joined me, and we sat looking at the water. I could hear field sparrows singing across the river, and a warbling vireo not far away in the willows, birds that would sing even on a warm afternoon. Putting them out of my mind, I tried to think of something to talk about.

Sure, I had read a lot of books — Charles Dickens, Mark Twain, James Fenimore Cooper, starting in on Dostoyevsky and Tolstoy. And in some of those, of course, men had talked to women with a certain degree of flair and confidence. I tried to recall some specifics. Compliments seemed to be good, but I mainly remembered the ones I hadn't understood. What did it mean if you told someone that her eyes looked like limpid pools?

Tamara broke the silence. "Did you see *The Avengers* last night?"

"Gee, no, I guess I missed it." Of course I had never watched it and was barely aware that the program existed, since we didn't even have a television in the house, but I didn't want to admit that right now.

"It was more of a funny story than usual," Tamara said, and started to describe the plot. I tried to listen dutifully, but bird voices in the distance threatened to distract me. A yellow warbler sang once or twice, and an orchard oriole. And farther away, far down the river, I caught the sound of some buzzy-sounding warbler song.

This spring I had been really working on learning more about the colorful, varied little birds called warblers. Up before dawn every morning, I had ridden my bike to various parks along the river to track down any warblers that had stopped over in migration. Up to twenty or thirty kinds of these little sprites were possible here, and since they were often hidden among the foliage, I wanted to learn to recognize their songs. They were all variable enough to make it a challenge. This buzzy song, now, I was sure it was a warbler, but which kind?

"Isn't that funny?" Tamara asked.

"Yeah, it sure is," I lied, not having heard a word of her account. "Must have been fun to watch. I'm sorry I missed it."

If only we had something in common to talk about! Tamara was as remote as the other girls in my classes, like an angel from another planet. We hardly seemed to speak the same language. I wanted to tell her what it was like to be here at the river at dawn, the first sunlight filtering yellow-green through the leaves, birds singing everywhere, stocky little green herons stalking intently along the bank. But I doubted I could describe it so she would understand. Could we talk about school? We had some shared experience there. But only yesterday she had made a mistake in front of the class and Mrs. Roberts had corrected her, and Tamara had just stood there, eyes down, color rising in her cheeks, while I'd desperately wished that I could come to her defense without inviting the ridicule of our classmates. No, she might not want to talk about school right now.

"What's your favorite TV show?" she asked.

Uh-oh, think fast. What was the name of that program I had watched over at Howie's place? "Well, *Star Trek* is good," I said. "If you like that sort of thing."

Down the river that interesting warbler sang again, just a little closer, and I stopped to listen. Must be a northern parula warbler, I thought. Buzzy tone quality, and the song rises toward the end. Northern parula was one of the uncommon but regular migrants in this region. This song didn't seem quite like the typical one, but their songs varied a lot, after all.

Tamara was playing with her long hair, twisting it around her fingers. "A couple of the girls were making fun of my hair yesterday," she said. "They told me it looked like the color of chicken noodle soup."

I felt an instant urge to protect her. "That's not true at all, Tamara," I said. "Your hair is a really pretty color. It reminds me of a buff-breasted sandpiper —"

"A what?"

"I mean — well, *buffy* isn't the right word, but it's a special color. It's really beautiful."

I hadn't noticed her moving, but now Tamara seemed to be sitting closer to me. "You really think so?"

"Absolutely," I said, gallantly. "Those other girls are just jealous of you."

Just then the buzzy-sounding warbler song came

again from downriver. Something about it sounded odd. Of course, there were other warblers besides the northern parula that sang buzzy songs, but their patterns were different. I should have known this by now. I'd been studying written descriptions, and listening over and over to my Peterson records with examples of a lot of these songs. Blue-winged warbler would just sing two flat buzzes. Black-throated green warbler would have about five distinct notes, nothing like this jumbled series followed by a rising buzz. What else could it be? Had to be just a funny parula...

Now cut it out, I told myself, pay attention to one thing at a time. Tamara was sitting close to me now, so close. Wow, was this the time that I was supposed to kiss her? I didn't know the protocol. It seemed like it would be dumb to ask first—"May I please kiss you" sounded totally dorky. Maybe I should just approach slowly, and that way she could back off if she wasn't ready. But first I had to get my courage up. She had seemed to like it when I complimented her, so I tried again. "Tamara, I'm sorry the other girls made fun of your hair. It's really beautiful. And your eyes, too, they're a wonderful blue, like...well ...like the blue of..."

Well, like the blue of what? Perhaps the blue of a cerulean warbler.

Holy cow! Maybe that was it! That odd warbler song— maybe it was a cerulean warbler! That would be a really great find here! I had never seen or heard a cerulean warbler, but this was pretty close to the descriptions and the one recording I'd heard, buzzy like a northern parula, with a different pattern: a few phrases on a lower pitch before the rising note. Could be tricky, though, because parulas have several song types. I needed to hear this one more clearly. If only it would come closer! If this really turned out to be a cerulean, it would be a find that all the local Audubon people would want to know about, and they would come to look for it, and they'd be impressed when they learned that I had picked it out by voice. I just needed to hear that song one more time —

Abruptly I realized that Tamara was no longer sitting next to me. She was standing, and starting to move slowly in the direction of her bicycle. "Well, I guess I should go do my homework," she said. "It looks like you're kinda distracted or something."

Time stood still. She was poised to leave but waiting, perhaps, for me to say something, and she looked so pretty that I could hardly stand it. I felt that I was close to something important, that the boundless wonder of the world was somehow near at hand and almost within reach. Life was so filled with mystery and magic. I had to say something.

"Sure, Tamara," I said. "See you in class tomorrow. Good luck with your homework." And I turned around to wait for the warbler to sing again.

The Name
of the Jar

"I've got it!" I said. "It must be a diabolical nightjar!"

Jeff Cox turned long enough to give me a look — one of his trademark looks, an expression of withering disdain for my comment, tempered somewhat by regret that he hadn't said it first. "You sound like a thirteen-year-old," he said, and went back to looking out the window.

I couldn't argue with that assessment. But I had a good excuse: I *was* a thirteen-year-old. For that matter, so was Jeff. We were intense young bird enthusiasts, keen teen birders, and as far as we knew, we were the only ones in town. Word had gotten out around the neighborhood that those boys knew something about birds, and grown-ups would sometimes ask us questions now, adding to our feeling that we had important knowledge.

But unfortunately for our budding careers as consulting ornithologists, right now we were looking at a bird we could not name.

"No, think about it," I persisted. "We could show Mrs. Thomas that quote from *The World of Birds*. Where Roger Tory Peterson says that hardly anything is known about the diabolical nightjar. We could say that people have been looking in the wrong place, looking in the mountains of Celebes, when there's this outpost population here in Wichita. She'd be totally thrilled."

"Yeah, and if the word got out, we'd get laughed right out of the next Audubon meeting. Although I doubt that any of those people have even heard of a diabolical nightjar. They won't have read the print off the pages of *The World of Birds* unless they're Peterson maniacs like you are."

Jeff had this irritating habit of being right most of the time. But I was still inclined to think that the bird in front of us could have been practically anything.

It was sitting on a low limb outside the window, as still as a feathery brown statue; Mrs. Thomas said that it had not moved in the two hours since it had caught her eye. We had to give her credit for spotting it at all. The bird was a study in camouflage, mottled and speckled and barred with brown and black and gray. Rather than perching in normal bird style, it was lying along the axis of a horizontal limb, feet tucked away under its body. Its wide, flat head ended at the front in a very short bill, half hidden by bristles; its huge eyes were narrowed to slits. It had a shadowy, brooding, introspective look, as if thinking of dark secrets and, yes, something diabolical...

And in reality, we had a basic idea what it had to be: a member of the nightjar family, a nighthawk or a whip-poor-will or a chuck-will's-widow. We had seen plenty of nighthawks — they probably nested on roofs somewhere in downtown Wichita, and they ranged over the suburbs and the surrounding countryside. We would see them on summer evenings, high overhead, jinking about with erratic beats of their long, angular wings. We also knew the whip-poor-will and chuck-will's-widow, even if we knew them mainly by sound. In the woods of Chautauqua County, we had heard their throaty chants night after night in summer. When we had pursued them with our little flashlights, we had merely seen dusky birds fluttering about, mothlike and batlike, their eyes dull embers in the flashlight beam. And we knew from our reading that there were related species, dozens of them, found all over the world.

So in a way we knew these birds, but only halfway. We had scant experience with nighthawks sitting down, or with whip-poor-wills or chuck-will's-widows in daylight. They were out on the periphery of our knowledge of birds. Hence our uncertainty about this still and silent bird in a Wichita backyard. If it had flown, or even stretched a wing, we could have seen whether it had the nighthawk's white wing patch; but as long as it sat still, it was just a mystery.

"One thing's for sure," Jeff observed. "We can't tell Mrs. Thomas that it's a nondiagnosable goatsucker. She'd call the police."

"Goatsucker," I said. "Yucch. What a word."

"Not our fault," said Jeff. "Blame it on the Ancient Greeks. Them again. Just when you start to get the language straightened out, here come those danged Ancient Greeks, tottering along, messing things up."

Jeff's irreverent rant was rooted in the facts. The name "goatsucker," as a group name for the nighthawk's kin, was based on a misconception that went back at least two millennia. In the pastures of the ancient Mediterranean world, goatherds would sometimes see a long-winged bird flying silently and low over the grass at dusk. The bird was the European nightjar — a relative of our whip-poor-will — and it was coursing through the pastures in pursuit of low-flying insects, but the ancients somehow got the idea that this stealthy, shadowy bird was there to steal milk from the goats. So durable was this myth that when formal scientific names were being applied to European birds, in the eighteenth century, this nightjar became *Caprimulgus*, the milker or suckler of goats. Its family has been the Caprimulgidae, the goatsuckers, ever since.

"Could have been worse," I said. "What if the Ancient Greeks had kept cows, mainly, instead of goats? We'd have a bunch of cowsuckers flying around."

"I'm so glad you decided to share that," Jeff said. "Actually, you know, they all have kind of weird names. The nighthawk obviously isn't a hawk. And those other names. Poor Will. Whip poor Will. Who's this Will character, anyway?"

He was kidding, of course, and he knew that the latter names were just transliterations of the birds' voices. But those voices could have been interpreted in other ways just as easily. I had heard the lonely whistles of the common poorwill; it was fair enough to write that call as *poor will,* but it also could have been written *hooh weeyew,* with an almost inaudible *jip* at the end. The husky cry of the chuck-will's-widow also could have been written *chook wheeyoh WEEthoh.* The chant of the whip-poor-will could have been written as *purrr-prr-RIPP.* Of course, all of those careful transcriptions would have been harder to remember and harder to write. Reason enough to stay with the traditional names.

But the point that stuck in my mind was the inclusion of the apostrophe in the official name of the chuck-will's-widow. That little punctuation mark made all the difference. It made that part of the name a possessive, and made it clear that these names were not just random syllables: they were phrases, strings of actual words. Chuck Will's widow indeed. Poor Will, we've whipped poor Will to death, and now we're going to chuck out his widow as well.

The phrases themselves were nonsense. What made sense was to use names that recognized these nightjars by their voices, because that undoubtedly was how they recognized one another, recognized their own kind. Even though their nighttime vision was better than ours, it seemed certain that they were not peering at one another in the dark and straining to make out distinctive markings among the mottling and barring and spotting of black and brown and gray...the way that we were, with this backyard mystery bird. No, they must have been going by silhouette and by sound, listening for those little gurgling and clucking noises of normal foraging, and for the distinctive, loud territorial chants of the males, the songs that humans would transliterate into words like "whip-poor-will."

Of course, to name a nightjar for its voice, you had to know its voice in the first place. The amateur ornithologist L. Irby Davis, one of the pioneers of sound recording of Mexican birds, had argued that the nightjars of the American tropics should be named for their sounds, just as their counterparts in North America were. So Davis had favored names such as the chip-willow. The pit-sweet. The cookacheea. The dusky cheer-for-will (the first hint, perhaps, that poor beleaguered Will was going to get a break). Unfortunately, in most cases, these more colorful and memorable terms had lost out to dry, dull, visually descriptive names — like tawny-collared nightjar or spot-tailed nightjar — describing details that generally could not be seen. Scientist names. In poring over the books, I had found only a few that seemed to have truly evocative or poetic names. The pennant-winged nightjar — an obvious name for the male, with his bizarre long black-and-white wing streamers, courtship accouterments that would show up in the dim light of the African dusk. The Nacunda nighthawk, of South America. Not to mention the diabolical nightjar, from the Kalabat Volcano in Celebes, wherever that was.

The weight of the authority for naming birds in the past had usually rested with museum scientists, comparing rows of stuffed specimens. Often, in the case of the nightjars, there were not many specimens for these museum authorities to use, despite the best efforts of the bird collectors. In the early part of the twentieth century, intrepid collectors were traveling the nether regions of the globe, shotguns in hand, scouring the tropical forests and deserts for those remaining birds that were still unknown to science. Understandably, the cryptic and elusive nightjars were often among the very last birds that they encountered. This scenario was repeated a number of times: a brown bird, disturbed in its daytime slumber, flutters up out of a thicket and into the crosshairs — *blam!* — to become a specimen that would lie in the museum tray for decades, even more cryptic in death than in life, spitefully guarding its secrets. Vaurie's nightjar. Cayenne nightjar. Prigogene's nightjar. One specimen only. Voice and habits unknown.

And if there were species of nightjars that were known from only a single museum specimen each, then it followed that there must be others that were known from no specimens at all — nightjars that were still unknown. Nightjars that were probably familiar to the hill tribes or the forest people in the regions where they lived but still uncataloged by the stuffy traditions of Western science. Nightjars with no scientific names and no English names. Unknown to science. The phrase had an exciting ring to it. Unknown to science...

"You come right down to it," Jeff said, interrupting my reverie and bringing me back to the present, "the name 'nightjar' is kind of funny, too. Night *jar*. What do jars have to do with it, anyway?"

I stared blankly. "Um, I have no idea."

"Mrs. Thomas, do you have a dictionary?"

"Goodness, Jeff! Yes, I do, but I don't think it will tell you about that bird."

Jeff brought the dictionary in. "Okay, here we go. Origin of the word...Hmmm...night plus jar. Gee, that's helpful. Oh, wait...Jar: to make a harsh sound."

"Is that all?" I asked. "Hmmh. So the European nightjar must have a harsh sound."

"Evidently," said Jeff. "At least it doesn't sound as harsh as the word 'goatsucker.' "

"Speaking of such things, how is the little sucker doing out there, anyway?"

Neither of us had been looking at it for the last few minutes. Now we both had the same thought at once and sprang to the window, but it was too late.

The bird was gone.

Of course: it had been evening when we had come

over to the house, and now the shadows were spreading, dusk was coming on. A bird of the night would be waking up, stretching, opening its big eyes, looking around furtively, and taking flight. It had slipped away while we were contemplating its name.

We slipped away ourselves, a few minutes later, promising Mrs. Thomas that we would report back after we did more research on her bird. ("Maybe a rare visitor from Celebes!" I said, while Jeff quietly kicked me.) In the lowering darkness outside, we could sense the presence of unknown nightjars — birds of mystery and wonder, birds with strange names, birds with no names — fluttering about in silence, just beyond the reach of human knowledge.

LOOKING BACK YEARS LATER, I know I never thought of myself as a selfish kid at the time. Yes, I had discovered this magical world of bird life, and no, I didn't say much about it to anyone, but I didn't give a lot of thought to my own motives. I wouldn't talk about birds to the kids at school, or to my brothers, very much, because I assumed they wouldn't understand. And I wouldn't talk to my parents much about birds, either. I told myself that they didn't have time to listen to this, but that was nonsense, because they always found time for us. I told myself that they wouldn't be interested, but I never tried very hard to find out if they would have been.

In fact, there was every reason to think that my parents would have shared my interest in birds and nature. My grandparents on my father's side, who passed away long before I was born, knew something about birds: my grandmother sometimes kept notebooks of her backyard bird sightings, while my grandfather found ways to mention birds in his newspaper columns. My mother's parents always had bird feeders up in the garden when she was growing up. Mom and Dad probably would have kept bird feeders, too, and it's possible that I was the reason they didn't. I was just so consumed by my obsession, so crazed about birds, that it left little room for anyone to take a more casual interest. I put up a bird feeder in the corner of the yard where it was hard to see from the windows; sometimes I would sit outside sketching the birds that came to the feeder, but more often I would fail to fill the feeder at all, thinking that I was a real birder who couldn't be bothered with mere backyard things. I kept weird hours, getting up before sunrise to prowl the neighborhood in search of migratory birds. I started inserting quotes from Roger Tory Peterson, the great bird expert, into conversations about unrelated subjects. I started memorizing scientific names, and if I ever deigned to mention what I had seen, I would toss off a casual "Oh, I was observing *Sturnella magna* and a flock of *Hirundo rustica*," instead of just saying that I'd been watching meadowlarks and swallows. All in all, in retrospect, the intensity of my focus on birds probably made me pretty obnoxious, so it was not likely that my parents would let their normal curiosity about the subject come to the surface while I was around.

As a young adult, I didn't go home much. I was living far away, struggling hard to make a living as a bird expert, so I didn't make it to my parents' house very often. By the time I was in my early thirties and I started making trips to see them again, I discovered something shocking: my parents were bird watchers. They didn't have binoculars, they didn't have a field guide, so they might have been a little hazy about what species they were seeing; but they kept a bird feeder filled right outside the kitchen window and enjoyed watching all the birds that came to visit.

My mother loved watching the cardinals, watching how the haughty demeanor of the brilliant red male was softened in early spring, when he began feeding the female in courtship. She was excited to have a brown thrasher that would sometimes venture out of the hedge to visit the feeder. She disapproved of the starlings, likening them to brash teenage hoodlums, but she thought of the house sparrows as simple children who could get away with occasional naughty behavior. And sometimes she thought she was seeing black-capped chickadees out in the yard, just a little too far away for a good look.

I could understand why she wanted to see chickadees. She remembered them from her childhood: tiny but spunky, just about as cute as a bird could be, but tough enough to keep bustling about with cheerful-sounding chatter on even the coldest winter days. They had been daily visitors to her parents' bird feeders in Iowa, so she didn't see why they shouldn't be in the backyard in Kansas also. But I knew better. Chickadees like big trees. There had been plenty of trees, apparently, in that Iowa town, big old trees planted two generations earlier, but there were none in our Kansas neighborhood. I knew that with certainty. As a kid I had scoured that whole sector of Wichita, on foot and by bicycle, and it was all relatively new subdivisions with no concentrations of larger trees anywhere. The nearest big trees and the nearest chick-adees were across the river in Herman Hill Park, three miles away. There was no reason why they would ever come to our yard.

I tried to break the news to my mother gently. She had only a vague recollection of what the chickadees look like, with their pattern of little black bib and black cap. Most likely she was seeing male house sparrows, which are not really similar but which do have a dark-capped, black-throated pattern. She might have been hurt if I'd suggested that, so I just said that a lot of other birds look sort of like chickadees and explained why we wouldn't have the real thing in that neighborhood. Mom wasn't inclined to argue with me, at least not openly, but she said she was going to keep watching for them just in case.

That had been several years ago now, and she had been watching for them ever since, right up to the time she had her stroke. Several times in her last years at home she had told me that she was almost certain she had seen chickadees, and each time I had patiently explained that that was impossible. And now that she was confined to this rehab center, she would still ask me if I had seen any chickadees when I had stopped by the house. I never said yes — I wasn't going to tell a white lie just to make her feel better. After all, my brothers and I still held to the hope that her condition would improve and she would go home again, and I didn't want her to go home expecting to see a bird that would not be there.

On this particular visit she had already asked me about the black-capped chickadees once, and we had had our usual conversation about why they wouldn't be there. Now she wanted to know about another type of bird that was a favorite of hers in a different way. "On this last... trip to South America," she asked, "did you see any flamingos?"

"Not this time," I said. "There are some in Venezuela but just at a few points on the coast. They weren't on our route. Actually," I continued, warming up to the subject, "three of the kinds of flamingos are up at high elevations in the Andes in southern South America. There are huge alkaline lakes there, in these wide valleys, high in the mountains, where the flamingos nest. Some of them come down to the Pacific coast as well."

"And of course...," Mom added, "there are flamingos ...on the Galápagos, too."

"Of course," I said, casting about quickly for a way to change the subject to something other than the Galápagos. "Actually, though, the most impressive flocks of flamingos I've ever seen are in Africa. I think I told you about Lake Nakuru after I went there the first time. Did I ever tell you about what happened when I went back a second time?"

Her brow furrowed in thought as she tried to remember. She wasn't sure. She asked me to tell her about it again.

A PAIR OF
SPECTACLES

WHEN I FIRST HEARD of Lake Nakuru, I was only ten years old. It was during a time when I was reading everything I could find by Roger Tory Peterson, my boyhood hero; when I ran across his account of Nakuru, it captured my imagination. According to Peterson's vivid description, this lake hosted "the greatest ornithological spectacle on Earth." And if the Master said so, it had to be true. Sitting in a humdrum neighborhood in the Midwest, I dreamed of Nakuru: half a world away, in Africa, a lake ringed by more than a million flamingos.

Years later I finally went to Kenya, and found Lake Nakuru to be as spectacular as Peterson had claimed. It was no exaggeration: the flamingos thronged the lake in staggering numbers. It was almost too much to take in, an overload for the eyes. Rank upon rank of flamingos, of two kinds — tens of thousands of greater flamingos, hundreds of thousands of lesser flamingos — crowded the shoreline and carpeted the shallows. They almost crowded the other birds out of view. Many other kinds of water birds were also present on Nakuru, present by the hundreds, but they were all but lost in the blaze of pink of the flamingo hordes. Lake Nakuru haunted my memory for weeks afterward, and I knew I would have to return.

But when I went back to Kenya for a second time, it had been five long years since my first visit, and I had heard disturbing rumors about Nakuru. It was said that the flamingo numbers there had dropped sharply, that the flocks were only thin remnants of their former abundance. The stories were distressing. Three friends were going along this time, two of them for their first visit to Africa. I knew they would be impressed with the wildlife of Kenya, of course; but for me, vicariously enjoying their first trip, it would not seem the same without the centerpiece of the Nakuru spectacle.

"Now, don't quote me on this," I confided to our driver, Orimba. We were sitting on the porch at one of the game lodges, having a drink at the end of a hot, dusty, wonderful day. "I'm not going to tell my friends, but I'm really disappointed to know that Nakuru won't be the same. It's a shame. Sure, we'll see some flamingos, but we won't see those fabulous numbers. It takes the best experience out of the trip."

Orimba smiled. He was a giant of a man from the western Luo tribe, towering above everyone else we met in Kenya, and he would have looked terrifying had it not been for his ready and infectious smile. "Maybe you worry too soon," he said. "Wait and see. Maybe your friends not be disappointed."

We each took another pull from our bottles of Bitter Lemon and stared out across the plains. I was not inclined to disagree with Orimba—not because he was twice my size but because he was a superb naturalist. He had had years of experience taking people to see the wildlife of East Africa. He must have been basing his statement on more than sheer optimism.

Still, I failed to make the connection a few days later, when Orimba insisted that we should make a side trip to Lake Bogoria.

We were staying at Lake Baringo at the time. A birdwatching itinerary in Kenya usually takes in a number of lakes in the Rift Valley; these alkaline lakes provide the water birds, of course, while various land birds range over the surrounding countryside. On this trip, Lake Baringo was the northern terminus of our route. The habitat around it offered our best chance for several dry-country birds, like Hemprich's hornbill and bristle-crowned starling. We needed to make full use of our short time here. Had it been up to me, I would have nixed the side trip to Bogoria. After all, what was there? A few greater kudus—one more kind of antelope we hadn't seen yet—and a few geothermal features. Hardly worth wasting half a day of birding time. On this trip, though, it was not up to me.

On my first trip around Kenya, two of us had traveled alone, renting a little four-wheel drive that we drove ourselves. Although we were occasionally lost, we eventually reached all our destinations, and we learned much of the country in the process. But on the current trip there were four of us, and we had chosen to hire a driver.

When you hire a driver in Kenya, you generally get more than a driver. Most of the safari drivers I've met there are talented individuals, able to converse in several languages, knowledgeable about the land and the wildlife, and remarkably patient with the demanding tourists. Some of the drivers are even super birders, able to sort out the dullest little birds and the subtlest call notes. Our man Orimba was not one of these, but he was a fine all-around naturalist. Every time we hit one of the game parks, other drivers would seek him out for advice. He knew enough that he often suggested destinations we would not have thought of on our own.

We soon settled into an ongoing, good-natured battle of wills. Will Orimba talk us into taking this unplanned side route? ("Should go there. Good chance see leopard.") Will we get Orimba to stop one more time for one more of those excruciatingly drab little African warblers called cisticolas? ("No can do. He fly away.") After a couple of days I was calling him King Orimba and he was calling me Cisticola Man, and we were all getting along fine.

But when Orimba started talking up Lake Bogoria, I guessed that I would be outvoted. All my protests about loss of birding time were to no avail. My friends, all cat lovers, were rightly impressed by the way Orimba had already shown us more big cats than we ever could have found on our own. And although my friends were keen birders, they were interested in all other aspects of nature as well. They were all swayed by Orimba's pitch about Bogoria: spectacular scenery, he said. Very unusual landforms. Fine animal, that greater kudu. And birds? Well, maybe some surprises.

So of course we went. I grumbled about it, but I went along, determined not to enjoy it very much.

We ran south on the good paved B4 through barren country and then off on a side road to the east, into an area with few settlements and little traffic. As we descended through low hills scored by rugged ravines, I was noticing how even here, in the dry season in dry terrain, the thorny scrub on the hillsides was mostly green. But not the green of a New Jersey woodland. Here in East Africa there are harsh, jarring shades of green that occur nowhere else on earth. *Hmm,* I said to myself, *I wonder if anyone ever checks this habitat. Could be all kinds of obscure birds lurking here, like Boran cisticola or even foxy cisticola*... "Wait a minute," I said. "My god. What on earth is that?"

But Orimba had seen it at the same time and had slammed on the brakes. "There he stands! The greater kudu!"

It was greater, all right. A large-boned, rangy animal, standing some distance off on a steep hillside, it seemed as big and regal as a horse. Each of its horns rose in an incredible spiral two or three feet above its shaggy head.

This was no wimpy gazelle or plodding, cowlike eland. In spite of myself, I was impressed. Although I'd been making fun of the creature's name earlier — talking about kudos for the kudus, and voodoo and hoodoo, et cetera, I had to admit that this was one animal worth seeing.

After we had watched the kudu for a while and taken some distant photos, we drove on, taking what seemed like a couple of unnecessary detours. Orimba seemed to be choosing his route with great care. It almost seemed as if he had chosen the timing as well: just as we broke out of the scrub and into a full, clear view of Lake Bogoria, a geyser erupted in front of us, white-hot water spewing thirty feet in the air. Steam drifted over us, and the smell of sulfur was heavy in the air.

And as the water subsided and the steam began to clear, we looked beyond it out onto the lake, and we gasped with astonishment.

The color pink does not occur commonly in nature. If we look through a manual of wildflowers, for example, we see that pink flowers are vastly outnumbered by those that are yellow or white. Pink birds are even scarcer. So we could hardly avoid feeling stunned when we were suddenly confronted by thousands and thousands and thousands of pink birds. The surface of Lake Bogoria was a seething mass of flamingos.

No matter how much you like the color pink, flamingos are not exactly "pretty" birds. Bruce Springsteen once recorded a song about a girl so good-looking that the boys called her "pretty flamingo." It sounds good in the song, or in theory, but it doesn't stand up to careful consideration. Picture a girl with grotesquely thin legs, a bizarrely bent beak, skinny neck, odd face, the very picture of potbellied anorexia. "Pretty" is not the word. "Striking," yes. Striking, impressive, arresting, remarkable. And, when seen in huge numbers, unbelievable. We could scarcely credit our eyes when we saw the huge numbers of flamingos spread out across the shallows of Lake Bogoria.

I turned to look at Orimba and saw that he had been waiting for my reaction. Now he roared with glee. "I told you, Cisticola Man! I tell you your friends not be disappointed!"

Suddenly I recalled something else I had read, years before, about how the flamingos move around from year to year in Kenya. Their flocks range up and down the broad Rift Valley, concentrating at whichever of the numerous lakes has the best conditions at the time. Usually that would be Nakuru. At the moment, evidently, it was Bogoria. It seemed possible that many of the flamingos missing from Nakuru had come here instead.

For the next three hours we worked along the edge of the lake, trying to take in the spectacle before us. In some places the shore was crusted with alkali deposits, and in some places steam rose from bubbling pools among the rocks. Everywhere the shallows were alive with flamingos. They were present by the hundreds of thousands, at least, defying our feeble attempts to make a serious count.

At close range, looking from the low angle of the lakeshore, we scanned through what appeared to be a forest of spindly red legs with pink bodies balanced on top. At any given time, thousands of the birds would be feeding — their necks hanging down like vacuum hoses, odd bills upside down in the water, straining the muddy soup of the lake bottom to filter out their tiny items of food. Others would be alert, heads held high, peering about, their necks moving in a reptilian fashion. The birds gabbled like geese, but seldom could we make out an individual voice; instead, the flocks made a continuous discordant murmuring.

We tried not to approach so closely as to frighten the birds, but sometimes they seemed nervous, walking slowly away from us, appearing almost to be marching in step. A couple of times we saw flocks take to the air, splash-running through the shallows with their wings beating furiously until they achieved liftoff. Often we saw distant flocks in flight. Lines and skeins would appear through the curtains of rising mist or trace patterns of shocking color against the dark hillsides. The flamingos looked just as unbelievable in the air as they did on the ground, incredibly long-necked and long-legged, shaped like lanky javelins, balanced on narrow wings. They seemed primitive and bizarre, creatures left over from some prehistoric experiment with flight.

The abundance of the flamingos was all the more striking because there were virtually no other birds present. It made for an otherworldly scene: stark surrounding hills, steam rising from the barren shore, geysers erupting from gurgling pools, not a living thing moving out there...except for the blaze of a million bright pink birds.

Later in the trip, of course, we did visit Lake Nakuru, and we found it amazing. I had not fully grasped, on my previous visit, just how many different species lived at Nakuru. Birds were swarming everywhere we looked: pelicans, storks, cormorants, grebes, herons, egrets, spoonbills, ducks, doves, plovers, sandpipers, gulls, terns, ibis, swallows, wagtails, and on and on, a dizzying display of diversity.

Oh, some flamingos were there, too — a few thousand. We hardly noticed them. The main image here, the overriding impression, was one of endless variety. It was a spectacle of a different kind.

OF ALL THE BIRDS that my mother would never get to observe, she had a special fascination with flamingos and penguins.

She never visited anyplace where there would have been wild penguins or flamingos, and I don't think she ever saw either type of bird in a zoo. If she had, she probably would have been disappointed at how small they were, because I think she imagined them to be much larger than they really are. Certainly they loomed large in her imagination, or in her view of the larger world outside her limited orbit in the American Midwest. These birds were so distinctive in pictures that she felt no doubt she would recognize one instantly if she happened to see a flamingo or a penguin out on the street. When I first started to travel internationally as a leader of birding tours, she always wanted to know if my destinations would provide any possibility of seeing flamingos or penguins.

It struck me as a singular coincidence that these same two groups of birds also had been the favorites of Roger Tory Peterson. Peterson, the author and artist and the inventor of the modern field guide, had been the world's best-known bird expert of the twentieth century. He had been my hero and role model since I was nine years old. From the time I had discovered his books and his magazine articles, as a little kid in the Midwest, his viewpoints had illuminated my view of the world, and I had been determined to grow up and follow him into the uncertain realm of freelance popular ornithology.

Raised in the early twentieth century, Peterson had conceived an idea for a pocket-sized guide to identifying birds, and he had written and illustrated it himself. Published in 1934, at the height of the Great Depression, his little *Field Guide to the Birds* had been an instant hit, launching a career that produced dozens of books, articles, and films, winning innumerable honors and awards. Peterson had not traveled much outside the United States until he was in his forties, but after that he had made up for lost time, visiting all seven continents repeatedly. At most destinations, Peterson would simply enjoy whatever birds were there, but he had made a special effort to see all of the world's varieties of flamingos and penguins. His trek to see the rare James's flamingo in the intermountain valleys of the high Andes had been covered in *National Geographic,* and he had arranged to get to remote islands south of New Zealand to see certain rare penguins. I found something uniquely intriguing in the fact that my mother, who knew nothing about birds, should have settled on the very same favorites as the world's number one birdman.

When my work as a bird-tour leader started to take me around the world, and I began to go back and describe these travels to my parents, my mother was particularly fascinated by tales of the Galápagos Islands. At first I thought maybe she was developing some curiosity about evolutionary theory, but it was nothing like that. She was dubious about that Darwin guy anyway, and not very interested in hearing about what had led him to formulate his ideas. Nor was she particularly curious about the giant land tortoises or marine iguanas on the islands, and she looked at me disapprovingly if I mentioned the blue-footed boobies there. No, she was fascinated with the thought that the Galápagos played home to both flamingos, which she thought of as tropical birds, and penguins, which she considered symbolic of the polar regions. She imagined these birds sitting side by side on the Galápagos in the ultimate twain-shall-meet combination.

It was true that both groups of birds were represented there. The Galápagos straddle the Equator, some six hundred miles west of the west coast of South America, and it is no surprise that strong-flying flamingos should have chanced upon the islands at some point in the past and established a colony there.

The presence of penguins might seem more surprising at first. However, despite the fame of those penguins that live in the frigid extremes of the Antarctic, most members of the family live in the South Temperate Zone. There are penguins along the coastlines of Australia and

New Zealand and South Africa, and all around the southern rim of South America, extending north along the west coast of that continent to Peru. The cold Humboldt Current, sweeping north off the coasts of Chile and Peru, surrounds the Galápagos with water that is shockingly chilly for their position in the center of the Torrid Zone; penguins must have come north with that current in ages past, to establish the family's northernmost outpost right on the Equator.

And somehow, the first time I talked to my parents about those Galápagos penguins, I left Mom with the impression that those birds could fly. I'm not sure how it happened. I know I had talked about all the odd creatures on those islands, probably mentioning that a type of cormorant living there was flightless — the only flightless member of this whole family of water birds. Perhaps I was unclear about that. Whatever the cause, my mother became convinced that Galápagos penguins, unlike all the other penguins in the world, were capable of flight.

When I realized that she believed this, I was in a quandary: should I correct her, or not? On earlier trips home I had been firm in correcting her mistake about chickadees in the backyard, insisting that no self-respecting chickadee would ever visit that relatively treeless neighborhood where my parents lived. She hadn't argued, but she might have been a little hurt by my insistence. On the penguin question, though, I wavered. Would it do any harm, after all, if I told a white lie by omission, letting her believe what she wanted to believe about these birds that were so far away? And after I had let this point go unanswered once, it became harder to go back and address the misconception later, so I just continued with this deception by default. Regardless of what books or TV documentaries might say, Mom believed that Galápagos penguins could fly, and she believed that she had that on the authority of her bird-expert son. So, uneasily, I just let it go.

Roger Tory Peterson had visited the Galápagos as a participant in a research expedition in the 1960s, and no doubt he had enjoyed the penguins and flamingos there, along with all the other birds and wildlife. Although Peterson had never had formal training as a scientist, he was universally respected as a bird expert in those days, and no one would have questioned his qualifications for taking part in a scientific expedition. That was several years before I met him for the first time. When I met Peterson, in the mid-1970s, I was a teenager and he was sixty-five. By that time, some of the young hotshot expert birders were starting to say openly that he was off his game, that he was no longer on the cutting edge of advanced birding. Caught up as I was, still, in hero worship for all that Peterson had accomplished, I ignored such talk at first. But gradually it began to affect my perceptions.

Somehow I had grown up thinking that all bird watchers everywhere would be instant friends, that everyone would unite around this common interest. I had no concept of the human propensity to form cliques and in-groups, to carry on petty conflicts and feuds. If I'd been paying more attention, I could have observed all that on the playground in grade school, of course, but back then I would have naively expected grown-ups to act more like adults. As an adult myself, though, I began to see that the community of bird watchers was far from being one big happy family. Differences of opinion, differences in approach, divided us as much as any other community. Upstarts who thought of themselves as the new experts might well try to discredit the authorities of previous generations, as a way of establishing their own credentials, so it was inevitable that Peterson's reputation should come under question eventually.

When I left Wichita at the end of that particular visit, my mind was filled with jumbled thoughts of my mother and penguins and Roger Tory Peterson. I thought of the young Turks in the birding world who felt that they had passed Roger by, pursuing the most challenging birds while he was still watching and photographing penguins. I thought of my mother's simple pleasure in simply thinking about penguins without even seeing them. I thought of my own reluctance to disillusion her about the Galápagos penguins and their fictional flying abilities, and I thought of how that reluctance would be incomprehensible to many of my fellow serious birders.

Most of all, though, I was thinking anew about the

challenge of communicating about this mysterious pursuit called birding. It was a challenge partly because we birders differed so much among ourselves in our approach. There were vast spaces between our versions of reality, how we perceived the birds, how we perceived one another, and particularly how we were perceived and understood—or not understood at all—by the outside world.

This Bird's for You

THE VOICE ON THE PHONE was unfamiliar, the message it conveyed was even more so, and it took me a minute to make the mental shift into this conversation. I had been at my drawing board all morning, illustrating the Arizona hummingbirds for a national bird magazine. Not the best way to prepare for discussions with a fast-talking, high-powered businessman from an advertising agency in New York.

"Mr. Kaufman," he said, "one of our clients is a beer distributor. And not any small brewery. We're talking big-time. I won't get into specifics, not yet, but this brand of beer is a household word." He paused, to give me time to be impressed, while I idly wondered about households that would include brand names of beer as subject matter for daily conversation. "We're lining up a new campaign," he went on, "and we're thinking of hiring you as a consultant. We're thinking of doing a TV commercial that features your sport."

A beer commercial. What a remarkable idea, I said to myself. I couldn't claim to know much about them, or about any commercials, because I had never watched television very much. A few times, however, I had watched sporting events on the tube: as televised, they had seemed to be long series of beer commercials, interrupted by occasional bursts of action on the playing field. So I had an overview of the genre.

The world depicted in the beer commercials was a world that was about 80 percent male. (Women in this world rarely got to speak any lines — they were ornamental, objects for stares and whistles.) The males were always doing masculine, manly things, like playing cards, fishing, teaching stupid tricks to their dogs, gawking at the silent women, and drinking gallons of beer. Sure, I knew the general themes.

"We're thinking of doing a TV commercial that features your sport," Mr. Ad Agency repeated, impatiently. "Do you think you'd be interested in acting as an adviser?"

"Yeah, sure," I said, thinking quickly. After all, it couldn't hurt. If even the beer dealers had come around to thinking about birding as a "sport," it must mean that the old stereotypes were fading away.

I thought about what life had been like for me as a teenage bird watcher. That was back in the 1970s, when the public image of birding had been purely cartoonish. Whenever I had seen bird watchers depicted in print then, they had been shown as little old ladies with blue hair and tennis shoes — or as befuddled old gentlemen with Bermuda shorts and pith helmets. They were always absurd caricatures. For a teenage boy, it had been tough to deal with that image, even though I knew it was false.

"Okay," said the Adman. "You realize this is just preliminary. Just a few questions. Is there some outdoor setting where we could shoot this, without having to send our people out too far from L.A.?"

It was obvious what kind of thing they wanted. The commercial would have to show tough male birders going out in tough surroundings to track down some rare bird, and then celebrating with the sponsor's beer.

Thinking of tough surroundings would be no problem. Plenty of our standard birding spots were tough enough. "Yeah, there are plenty of rugged places we go to, here in the Southwest. The problem will be figuring out one where your filming crews can get in without too much difficulty."

I thought about Sycamore Canyon in Arizona, that nine-mile-round-trip scramble over rocks and across sand and through thorny thickets, where the birder faces the alternate threats of dehydration and flash floods, with rattlesnakes and searing heat thrown in for good measure. Sycamore Canyon was where we had invented the statement "The Marines are looking for a few good birds." Sycamore Canyon on a hot day would entice even a teetotaler to sample the sponsor's brew. But there was no way we could get any camera crew from Los Angeles down into Sycamore.

Then I thought about Painted Rock Dam. It's not far from Gila Bend, which often posts the hottest official reading in the country—but only because no official reading is taken at Painted Rock itself. On trips there, birders may struggle along the ragged shoreline, among the skeletons of the mesquites drowned by the rise and fall of the reservoir, with no trace of shade for miles. But again, no one could persuade any advertising film crew to get out to the best (worst) areas. However, the idea of Painted Rock Dam touched off another...

"Salton Sea," I said. "That's the place. You can get your footage there."

There was silence on the other end, so I went on. "It's in southern California. It can be pretty rugged in summer, when the humidity's over 90 percent, and the temperature hits a hundred before eight in the morning, and the water in the sea seems pretty lethal with all the salt buildup and all the chemicals that have washed into it. But your cameramen could ride out there in air-conditioned vehicles—there are a few decent roads—and then they could get out just long enough to do their filming. They'd probably survive."

The New York adman sounded a little more hesitant. "I've, uh, never seen you people in action." I wasn't surprised; he sounded as if he'd never seen a bird, let alone a bird watcher. "*Is* there any action that would work well in close-ups?" he asked. "Or any dialogue that would fit into a commercial?"

"Sure!" I said. "Plenty of it." I could see it now. You could show a bunch of guys — four or five macho-looking real birders, ranging in age from early twenties to early fifties, much as you might find in a real carload of guys going out for a weekend of birding. Show them shouldering their scopes and heavy tripods and sloshing out into the tepid water of the Salton Sea, steam rising around them from the knee-deep ooze, sweat running down their backs as they trek across the shallows toward a frigatebird perched in the stark remains of a drowned tree. Then cut to their triumphant return, cracking open the ice chest and guzzling cans of the sponsor's brew, while they kid one another with words of manly camaraderie.

It would make a fine commercial — and it would help the young male birders of today, who still might be smarting under a lingering notion that birding is an activity for "sissies."

And why stop at one commercial? There were plenty of possibilities. "After a tough day birding at the sewage ponds, you deserve an ice-cold beer." "After you've climbed the mountains of garbage at the dump and seen the slaty-backed gull, then comes beer time." We could fill the TV screens with images of macho birders — tough, manly men, swaggering through the field, finding birds and drinking beer. The possibilities were endless. "Yes sir," I said out loud. "Birding could be the best thing that ever happened to your client's beer."

"What?" said the Adman. "Birding? What do you mean?"

"Birding. You know. My avocation. My sport, as you put it. What you want to feature in your commercial."

The voice on the phone was suddenly almost shrill. "Birding? Bird watching? You're kidding me. Aren't you the guy from the monster wheels mud racing competition?"

"No, actually, I'm a bird watcher —"

The last thing I heard from the Adman was half of a muffled profanity, ending in a click, as he hung up on me.

Feeling unsettled, I put down the phone and walked slowly downstairs. So there would be no birding beer commercial after all. Apparently we birders were still not masculine enough to suit the dictators of taste on Madison Avenue. What would it take, I wondered, to convince these advertisers that male birders are Real Men? Would we have to study the beer commercials and slavishly follow the examples set there? Would we have to roar out into the boondocks in monster trucks, drinking gallons of beer and burping and gawking at female birds to create a macho stereotype?

But then again, I said to myself, *perhaps it didn't matter.* Why should anyone let his actions be dictated by advertising? Maybe the Real Men, and the Real Women as well, were those people who did what they pleased without worrying about stereotypes. Turning this over in my mind, I wandered into the kitchen and opened the refrigerator.

A label caught my eye: there, in the back of the bottom

shelf, was most of a six-pack of beer. We had bought it a month or two earlier when friends had come over, and we had never finished it. Mesmerized, I stared at the ice-cold bottles, replaying in my mind the commercials that would not be.

Then I poured myself a glass of iced tea. Feeling tough and manly, swaggering just a little, I went back upstairs to finish my hummingbird drawings.

SUPERCOOL

THE LEAVES MOVED AGAIN, and the bird hopped into the open. It was a warbler — a tiny bird, just a few inches long, and just a few feet away from me. It was so delicate and so intensely alive that it would have been beautiful to watch even if it had been plain gray, but it was far from plain. The black feathers of its wings and tail were set off with crisp edges and patches of white, and broad creamy stripes ran down its black back. Its chest and throat were orange — a striking, glowing, brilliant orange. Up on the bird's face, where this color wrapped around a narrow black mask, the effect was even more intense: it deepened to a fiery orange, burnt orange shade, and . . .

And just then I heard a voice right behind my ear: loud but weary, resigned, vaguely depressed, a voice that was absolutely dripping with tired boredom. "Oh," said the voice. "It's just another blackburnian warbler."

Even as I was turning around to look, I recognized the accent and knew what I would see: four young British birders, perhaps in their early twenties, making their first trip to North America. They had been touring Texas for the last two weeks, and our routes had intersected several times. Now they stood behind me on the trail through Smith Woods in High Island, Texas, shuffling their feet and looking about at the sunlight streaming through the old oak trees. "So sorry," one of the guys said, with an apologetic shrug. "We thought maybe you were looking at something *good.*"

The first response that came to my mind was, Sorry yourself, I didn't know the blackburnian warbler was *bad*! But I resisted the temptation to say it out loud. For a moment I couldn't think of anything to say, and I just looked at them blankly.

We had had enough contact already that I knew they were nice enough, courteous and pleasant in conversation. They knew who I was — they had a copy of my *Field Guide to Advanced Birding* along, although of course they would not be caught dead actually reading it, or reading any field guide — and whenever our paths had crossed during these last two weeks, they had sidled up casually to engage me in discussion of birds. Their approach focused on two recurring themes: pumping me for advice on birds they had not yet seen while expressing boredom with the things they *had* seen. "Oh, yes, we saw the golden-cheeked warbler. It was easy. (yawn) But now what about this Canada warbler, eh?" And so on . . . all the while putting on a who-cares attitude, a studiously casual air.

Just another blackburnian warbler indeed, I thought. How could they say that? They had all told me this was their first visit ever to the Americas, and the blackburnian warbler was an extremely rare visitor to their side of the Atlantic — there had been only a couple of records ever in Britain. Surely they had all seen their first blackburnian within the last couple of weeks. How could it slide to old-hat status so quickly? But still I could think of nothing to say, so I stalled for time. "Oh, hi. How's it going? Seeing anything interesting?"

The most talkative of the group, a dark-haired guy who usually seemed to act as their spokesman, shrugged his shoulders and looked at the ground. "Oh, not really. It's been quiet. Seeing all the thrushes today, of course, and all the usual migrants. Not much luck." His three companions all nodded, shrugged, with their hands in their pockets and dour expressions on their faces. The blackburnian warbler was still out in the open, but they hardly glanced at it.

Memories came crowding back to me, memories of other times that I had seen blackburnian warblers. I thought of the very first one I'd seen, when I was a kid in Kansas, a glowing little flame on a gray May morning. I thought of days in the migration seasons, days in spring and fall when there had been "fallouts" of blackburnians and other warblers, filling the trees with movement and life. I thought of places where I had seen them on their nesting grounds, such as forests of Quebec, where the males perched atop dark spruces to sing their buzzy, wiry phrases. Sure, I had seen this species many times, but I couldn't imagine taking it for granted.

Just then a movement caught my eye: in a nearby elm, a male rose-breasted grosbeak was hopping along a branch, his neat pattern of black and white and rose red standing out against the pale green leaves. One of the British birders — a tall, thin lad, seemingly a bit younger than the rest — raised his binoculars to look at it. Right away, one of his friends asked, a little sharply: "Got something there, Steven?"

"No," said Steven, hastily lowering his binoculars again. "Just checking to see if it was second-year or third-year."

All at once I thought I understood what was going on, and how their peer pressure must be working. These guys were keen birders — no question about it. They wanted to be accepted for the knowledge and skills they undoubtedly had. They did not want anyone to think they were just beginners. Beginning birders would get excited about common birds, of course, seeing them for the first time; so how could these guys prove that they were not beginners? By *not* getting excited about common birds. And just to be on the safe side, just in case any of these birds might be common someplace, these birders would not get visibly excited about anything at all.

Perhaps their need to be totally cool was increased because they were on unfamiliar ground. A few years before, some wide-eyed American commentator had planted the idea that British birders were more skilled, on average, than those of this continent. It wasn't true, of course, but it placed more pressure on any birders who came over from Britain: they had to keep up appearances. For my four new friends here, the pressure must have been intense. Here in the rip-roaring wilds of Texas, they had to look experienced and cool at all costs.

This casual, bored approach was not an essential part of the British birding model. I knew that, because I had had the good fortune to go afield with the late Peter J. Grant of England, one of the world's great authorities on field identification. Peter had had no qualms about showing his enthusiasm for birds. One time in Alaska, he had spent ten minutes watching a male pine grosbeak that was feeding at eye level in front of us. It was not a rare bird, it was not at all hard to identify; he said he was watching it because it was so beautiful.

Still, many younger birders from Peter's country seemed to take on an affectation of boredom when they were in groups. And I had seen the same thing in other places. It was something that happened — not always, but often — in regions with lots of expert birders.

On this continent, I had seen the phenomenon of birder boredom most often in California. That state has a high percentage of America's top birders; in terms of expertise, California often leads the nation. And the real experts there are hardly bored or boring. Consider the great Rich Stallcup, a man with extraordinary depth of knowledge about birds. If you go out in the field with him, the big thing you notice is not the fact that he knows a thousand times more than you do (even though he does); what catches your attention is the fact that Rich really loves birding. For example, I recall a time when several of us were looking at an American redstart that was flitting about in some willows. After everyone else had lowered their binoculars, Rich Stallcup was still watching it. "Come on, Rich," one of his friends said. "You've seen redstarts before."

"Yes," said Rich, agreeably. "But I hadn't seen *this* one."

Unfortunately, many California birders — wannabe experts, perhaps — do not appreciate their birds so openly. The search for rare finds is the big thing (or even the only thing) for many, and common birds become part of the background, an annoyance to be ignored while one searches for the next rarity. It seems the ultimate goal is to find several rare birds, so that one can casually list them off in conversation, with a look of utter boredom. The underlying message is, Yeah, I saw all these rare species, but I'm such an expert that I can't possibly get excited about birds like that.

If birders are just playing one-upmanship among themselves, each trying to look more bored or casual than the next, it may not do any harm. But it's a bad approach to take with strangers. One time in Arizona I was birding a marshy area called the Arivaca Cienega, and I found a green heron poking along the edge of a creek; it was a young bird, beautifully marked, with crisp white spots and pale edgings on all its wing feathers. While I was watching it, an older couple that I didn't recognize came bustling up behind me. The woman, in the lead, asked me imperiously: "Have you seen anything good?"

"Um...nice green heron here," I said.

The woman fixed me with a cold glare. "It's called green-*backed* heron," she said, "and it's a *common bird.*" She and her silent companion swept away haughtily down the trail.

I didn't know whether to laugh or be angry. The woman was almost right on both counts; the bird *had* been called "green-backed heron" for a time, and its name had been officially changed to "green heron" just a few years before this encounter. And yes, green herons are fairly common birds across most of North America. But what if she had had this mini-conversation with a brand-new birder? What if this had been my very first green heron, and my excitement had been crushed by this casual dismissal? How could anyone be so thoughtless?

I thought of another encounter, this one in South America, where I had been leading a birding tour. On the slopes of the Andes we had run across a mixed flock of birds in the forest: golden tanagers, blue-necked tanagers, bay-headed tanagers, and more than a dozen other species, a giddy kaleidoscope of tropical colors. We were all enjoying these birds — all of us except one man, who was in single-minded pursuit of more birds for his life list. Every time a new species popped up, we could practically see the numbers clicking in front of this man's eyes. At one point he grabbed my arm impatiently. "What's this little bird?" he demanded, gesturing at the treetops.

"Oh, that's great," I said. "Blackburnian warbler. They spend the winter here, with these mixed flocks. Neat to think of them migrating all this distance."

The man stared at me with disgust and anger. "Listen," he said. "I didn't come all the way to South America to look at a damned blackburnian warbler."

A couple of days later, one of the women in the group told me that that had been her first blackburnian warbler ever. Her enjoyment of it had been spoiled, in large part, by our bored lister, who had shown such contempt for the blackburnian, even though he had been unable to recognize it.

My mind had been drifting, but I was brought back to the present by a comment from the British birders. Their nominal leader had been listing off some of the things they'd seen. "Of course we've ticked off most of your warblers ... including most of the ones that are rare this far west, like Cape May and blackpoll. We haven't seen a black-throated blue warbler, but that seems pretty unlikely —"

"Actually," I interrupted, "you're right, the black-throated blue is scarce this far west. But I did just see one half an hour ago."

The listlessness of the Brits suddenly morphed into a rabid intensity. *"What? You did? Where was it?"*

"Just down here where the trail goes through a turnstile and breaks out into the open — then around to the right about twenty yards, where there's no undergrowth under the oaks. Beautiful adult female."

They were galvanized. "Come on, lads!" cried one of the birders, and they were off, practically running down the trail, failing utterly in their attempt to act cool and sophisticated.

Well, I thought, so much for their apparent boredom. These guys were going to be all right. Eventually they would get past their current supercool phase and let themselves become openly excited about the birds they saw. For the time being, they were just responding to peer pressure, acting out a quirk of human behavior.

Sometimes, I reflected, the birders could be just as fascinating to observe as the birds. I smiled and turned around, and went back to watching the blackburnian warbler.

HELL'S BIRDERS

IT WAS A MEANDERING dirt road, a deserted road, that traced the edge between two worlds: on one side a wide marsh, open to the sun, and on the other a shady forest where the first fall colors were just beginning to show. Birds were mostly quiet on that September morning, and most of my attention was focused on scanning the marsh. But of course I was listening, too. It was an instinct, born from years of birding, to listen at all times and make a mental tally of all distant sounds: Carolina wren. Brown thrasher. Yellowthroat. Titmouse. Blue jay. Motorcycle.

... Motorcycle?

Yes. No, make that plural. Several motorcycles. Distant, but coming my way.

Of course you understand that I have nothing against motorcycles. I have no problem with the fact that two of my brothers ride them. Rick and Ralph are both clean-living, hardworking, intelligent men, worlds away from any negative image that might be conjured up by the word "biker." Ready reminders, if I should ever need reminders, that false stereotypes should be ignored. Still, I was being approached by a dozen-plus motorcycles, all ridden by large, hairy men with leather vests and wild expressions, and it seemed only prudent and courteous to step out of their way.

By the time I had looked up, they were closer than they sounded — practically up to where I was standing. Resisting a sudden impulse to go off looking for birds deep in the woods, I merely stepped off the road into the weedy margin. But the bikers pulled up and stopped right next to me.

I am not one of those who can recognize motorcycle brands on sight, by their field marks. But I could see the insignia on tanks or fenders of several of these bikes: Harley-Davidsons. Big, powerful cruisers, with long, low-slung exhaust pipes, flared handlebars, throbbing engines, surfaces of gleaming leather and chrome. American classics. The only thing that seemed odd was how quiet they were, almost as if the engines had been specially adjusted for low volume.

The guys riding the bikes looked the part of American classics, too. Motorcycle boots, faded jeans, wide leather belts, leather vests with chains, bandannas, sideburns or beards, sunburns, sunglasses. The guy at the front of the pack appeared to be the biggest and baddest of the lot. He had wild black hair that was thinning on top, and he had a screaming eagle tattooed on one brawny arm. I realized that he was staring at me quizzically: "What are you seeing?"

I missed the nuance of the question, if there was any;

maybe I was still distracted by wondering why the bikes were so quiet. "I'm, uh, looking for birds," I said.

A couple of the bikers started to laugh. The big guy cut them off with a sharp glare before turning back to me. "Thanks a lot, chump. Guess I look like an idiot today. What *kinds* of birds are you seeing?"

"Migrating birds," I said. "Warblers. Thrushes. Vireos. Sandpipers. They're little birds, but they fly a long distance — a lot of them are heading for the tropics."

He interrupted me. "Yeah, I know. You seen any Connecticut warblers?"

My mouth must have dropped open, and I stuttered for a response. But the big biker was impatient. "What ya looking so surprised for? They do come through here, ya know."

One of the other bikers spoke up. "Aw, forget it, Caveman. Looks like this dude wouldn't know a Connecticut if it bit 'im."

I was moved to protest. "Yeah, I would. I've seen Connecticut warblers in fall. Real ones, not just young mourning warblers with eye-rings."

"Oh, so you do know something," said the big guy. He looked at me narrowly. "Wait a minute — you look familiar. I seen your picture. You write stuff for the bird magazines. Kaufman, right? Hey, we got almost the same name. I'm Caveman."

"Uh, pleased to meet you," I replied.

"And this here's Badger, and that's Miko, and that's

Doc, and Catbird..." He introduced them all, names all sounding like aliases. "We're the Thrashers." They had all shut off their motorcycle engines by now and pulled out good binoculars that had been tucked into padded pockets on their vests. Even as we talked, various members of the gang were scanning the marsh or looking around at the treetops.

My mouth was still hanging open in surprise, and I tried to collect my wits. "Well, I'm glad to know you," I said. "I've never heard of a, um, er, ah" — I was suddenly wondering whether the term "biker gang" was considered polite — "I've never met a group of birders quite like you."

They were looking at me in silence, inscrutable behind their dark glasses, so I tried again. "So, you were all in this, um, motorcycle club together, and then you all got interested in birding at the same time?"

"No, we were mostly birders first, separately," said a grizzled-looking character, the one called Badger. "And then we just sorta came together through shared interest. From different backgrounds. I was a loner. Miko here used to ride with the Satan Cycles."

My expression must have changed, because Miko, a red-haired young man with rattlesnake tattoos on both arms, hastily clarified this. "That's just a name, you know, they ain't Satan worshipers. Most of them ain't really bad dudes, long as nobody crosses 'em. They just like to be left alone is all. Sometimes we started some trouble, but I think it was just because we was bored. Wanted something different. I was bored to tears sometimes before I fell in with the Thrashers."

"Yeah," one of the other bikers chimed in. "We picked him up when we went to look at that long-billed murrelet."

"Yo, man. I couldn't believe it. Little pond in Ohio, and here's this funny little seabird that's supposed to be on the coast of Siberia. I thought you guys was messing with my head. Wasn't even in the field guides you had along 'cause it had just been split from marbled murrelet."

I pinched myself, convinced that this had to be some bizarre dream, but I didn't wake up. Questions crowded my mind. Despite their rough appearance, these guys did not seem violent, so I ventured to ask: "Excuse me, but I'm curious. The general public has certain ideas, stereotypes, about bikers — um — about motorcycle enthusiasts who ride around in groups. And the public has certain stereotypes about bird watchers. And I'm sure you realize that those public images are really, really different. So I can't help but wonder. Does it seem unconventional to you guys to be combining these two activities?"

"You tell the man, Doc," said Caveman, swiveling around to one of his henchmen. "You've got the words. Doc is our philosophy man," he added, directing this to me.

"Look you here," said Doc. He was a thin black man with wraparound dark glasses, and he had been sitting quietly off to the side. "Consider. The Harley is a thing of beauty, is it not?" He slapped the side of the bike that he was straddling, and I nodded agreement, seeing no reason to argue. "A machine of sleek lines and power. Why is it shaped thus? Pure chance? Random choices? Not at all. Form follows function. Structure is dictated by reality. The reality of wind resistance and the force of two wheels turning against pavement. It is shaped by the laws of aerodynamics and gravity and acceleration."

In the background, a couple of the guys were murmuring, "That's it" and "You tell 'im, Doc." Then someone called out, "Hey! Broad-wing coming over." A young broad-winged hawk was coming along the edge of the woods, kiting above the treetops, gliding and circling. We all stopped and watched until it disappeared behind the trees.

Doc smiled and went on. "Now consider again. The bird. Why is it shaped thus? Pure chance? Of course not. What other shape would fly so well? When the Big Guy in the sky was designing the birds, He tooled them up in accordance with His laws of aerodynamics and gravity. A bird is a thing of beauty because it functions so well, and vice versa. In its own way, a broad-winged hawk is almost as perfect as a Harley-Davidson."

I couldn't think of a single thing to say in response, but fortunately another biker spoke up. "You watch a peregrine falcon in flight, speeding through the sky, free and clear, with the wild wind in its face.... Besides the birds, who knows that feeling? We do. That's what it's like on a bike on the open road."

"And talk about attitude, man!" said another. "Does anybody tell them birds what to do? Do they give a hoot about any speed limits? No way! They come to a border, they just fly on across, never mind any customs or immigration."

Another man spoke. "You walk up to an eagle or a great blue heron, he'll pick up those big wings and fly away. Is he scared of you? Not a chance. Just wants to be left alone is all."

"Just like us," another man added.

"Yeah, the birds do whatever the hell they want," said another guy. "Don't matter what the books say. The books all say that fork-tailed flycatcher is a tropical bird, but hey, *we* found one on the coast of Maine last month!" All the guys whooped and pumped their fists in the air.

I was still shaking my head, mentally, with disbelief. "Yes, that's rare, all right," I said. "But the rarest thing around here is you guys. I never would've believed it. There isn't any other, um, bird club that comes close to this one."

A couple of the guys started to laugh, but then Caveman held up his hand. "Listen!"

We all listened.

"Downy woodpecker?" said one man.

"Indigo bunting?" said another.

"No," said Caveman. "I mean, yeah, those are out there, but—Listen again."

And now we all heard it. More motorcycles. Distant, but coming our way. "Sounds like Hondas," Doc mused, and several guys nodded.

Uh-oh, I thought, what do other bikers do when they find out about a gang of birders? I thought about the prejudice I'd encountered in the past, all the way back to grade school and so many times since, from ignorant people who thought that bird watching was for "wimps" or "dorks." How would bikers respond to having that false stereotype mingled with their own? And as the sunlight glinted on a fleet of cycles coming around a distant corner, it occurred to me that maybe I was about to find out.

Most of the guys had their binoculars up, looking. "It's them, all right," said Caveman.

"You know these guys?" I asked.

Caveman laughed. "Yes and no. They ain't guys. Them's the Titmice."

"The . . . the what?" But no one was paying any attention to me now. I stepped closer to Miko, the red-haired biker. "Why a name like Titmice?"

"Because they're birders," he said impatiently.

"Come on! You're telling me there's more than one birding biker gang?"

"Aw, there's several," he said. "There's the Wayward Woodpeckers, and the Dangerous Dunlins . . ." But the other bikers were practically up to us now. Half a dozen tough-looking young women, riding big Hondas, bikes that — again — seemed oddly quiet for their size. The guys were glaring, the women looked defiant, there was tension in the air.

The woman riding in the lead came to a stop and took off her helmet, and long blond hair spilled across the shoulders of her leather jacket. "So, Caveman!" she said. "Out of gas?"

"Something you'll never be," Caveman said derisively. "So, Spunky, are you Chickabirders having a good time here on *our* turf?"

A couple of the women scowled and muttered insults, but the one called Spunky just laughed. "You're still pissed off because we found that black-tailed godwit before you did. Don't worry — someday you'll figure out how to find rare birds. But hey, get this. We want your help. We just found a gull." There was a noticeable shift in the expressions on the bikers' faces. "I know that you and Doc and Badger spent time in Oregon a couple of winters ago, studying gulls. We're honestly not sure what this bird is. It could be a slaty-backed gull. We need a second opinion."

"Slaty-back!" cried Badger. "That'd be a first state record!"

"Only if we can prove it," said Spunky. "Suzanne and Bitsy are back there watching it now. Maybe five miles from here. Will you come with us and take a look?"

Instantly the motors were revved up, the bikes were swinging around on the road, the leaders were starting to peel out toward the horizon — and I realized that I'd left my car parked half a mile up the road in the other direction. "Wait!" I yelled. "Where's the gull?" One of the women shouted something back at me; it sounded like directions, but I didn't catch it all. By the time I had jogged back to my car, the bikers were long gone.

For the next couple of hours I drove all the roads in the area, looking for them and for their mystery gull. Scattered gull flocks were around, but there was no sign of the bikers; they seemed to have vanished into the air, almost as if I had imagined them. Eventually I had to give up. Musing about the experience, I drove on down the coast.

At the outskirts of the next large town, a storefront sign caught my eye: ALL AMERICAN CYCLES. Several gleaming new motorcycles were parked out front, and through the window I could see rows of others inside the store. On a sudden impulse I pulled into the parking lot.

Well, why not? I asked myself. In its own mechanical way, a motorcycle might be almost as perfect as a broadwinged hawk. It wouldn't hurt to look.

But first, I needed to be properly attired. I dug around in the back seat for my cap with BIRDER'S WORLD blazoned across the front, pulled on my Tucson Audubon Society T-shirt, put on my vest with the American Birding Association patches, and slung my binocular strap around my neck. *Down with stereotypes,* I said, and sauntered in to look at the motorcycles.

ON ONE OF MY VISITS to Wichita to see my parents, I had been filled with a new zeal for accuracy, probably as a side effect of work that I had been doing as an associate editor of an ornithological publication. Weeks of fact checking and copyediting and correcting had put me in a frame of mind where I was determined to weed out any error, stamp out any misconception. On that trip, I had it in mind that I was going to tell my mother the truth about the Galápagos penguins: that those birds really could not fly. I would break it to her gently, I reasoned, and she wouldn't mind so much, especially if I told her how graceful the penguins were in the water. They could fly through the depths of the sea with all the speed and precision of fish, I would tell her, so it was no great tragedy that they could not fly through the air. That was what I had planned to tell her, anyway, if the subject of the Galápagos penguins came up in conversation.

But that was the visit when I first became fully aware of the health problems she was having. Her arthritis had gotten far worse, and she had developed curvature of the spine, bad enough that it was going to require surgery. She felt awkward and self-conscious about it, but as always she tried to put on a brave face, even joking about her condition. The only reference to penguins on that visit was her grim joke that she was becoming more penguinlike herself, getting shorter all the time, waddling instead of walking. I dared not say anything discouraging about penguins myself, so I just let it go.

It was on that visit, too, that I first began to understand that the strength of her spirit was not tied to bodily strength; even as her physical health began to deteriorate, she remained as strong-willed as ever. As kids, my brothers and I had never thought of that very much, because our father had been such a tower of strength. Physically, mentally, emotionally, he was gentle but powerful, with strength of character that never wavered. Those things were obvious to us when we were young. Later we came to understand that in her own way, aside from the physical part, Mom was a lot like him. Forget the line about opposites attracting: Dad never would have been attracted to a weak woman.

They must have made such a striking couple when they first met at college. Dad was an engineering student, twenty-two years old, back from serving in postwar Europe and going to school on the G.I. Bill. My mother couldn't help but notice how handsome he was, with his aquiline profile (a result, she found out later, of his nose having been broken in a fistfight while he was in the army) and blue-gray eyes. He couldn't help but notice her, a slim, dark-haired, nineteen-year-old beauty, with hazel eyes that flashed when she laughed, which was often. She was majoring in drama, with a minor in English literature. So while his classes focused on the scientific and mathematical, hers were centered on the artistic and literary. Perhaps something about opposites applied after all. Whatever the reasons, they were soon dating, and eventually engaged, and then married, living in a tiny apartment, Mom going to work to support them while Dad finished the last year of his engineering degree.

As a child, my mother had no ambitions beyond wanting to win the approval of her stern father, but after she went away to college and began to study drama in a serious way, she dreamed of starring on Broadway, seeing her name in lights. She put that dream away — happily, she always assured us — when she got married. After my father graduated and got his first real job, at Bendix, she went with him to the cold winters of northern Indiana, starring in a permanent role as a wife and mother.

It was pointless for me, looking back through the lens of my own experience and ambitions, to try to judge what this meant to her, what she had given up and what she had gained. She told us lightly that she still had outlets for creativity: designing elaborate sets for the company Christmas shows at Bendix and later at Boeing, decorating the most fanciful birthday cakes, showing the Cub Scouts how to make the most remarkable crafts.

And then she found an outlet for her drama training as well. Through a family connection she volunteered to read entire books into a tape recorder as part of a books-for-the-blind program. She took this work seriously, finding a quiet part of her day to sit and read aloud, in a clear, precise voice, a chapter at a time. I remembered being deeply impressed when she was reading a biography of Bertrand du Guesclin, the medieval French military hero; Mom went to great lengths to research and pronounce correctly all of the French names for people and places, sometimes recording a whole chapter three or four times over until she was sure she had done it flawlessly.

Now those days were long past. It was so hard for her to speak, but she still struggled gamely to make conversation as well as she could. She was tired, it was obviously making her tired to have my company all day. But when I suggested that I could leave for a while so she could take a nap, she begged me not to go. "Please . . . stay a little longer. Tell me more about the birds you saw. On your trip. Or tell me what you're writing. Are you still writing?"

"Yeah, actually, I am," I said. "I'm still doing that column for *Bird Watcher's Digest*." That gave me an idea. I had been struggling to come up with more things to talk about, to keep my mother's mind occupied so she wouldn't focus on the discomfort she was feeling. Those written columns would give me material to keep things going for minutes at a time, allowing her to rest and listen. Just as she had once read for the blind, now I could read to her.

I had brought my laptop computer into the rehab center with me, not wanting to leave it out in the rental car, and printouts of several columns were stuffed into the outside pocket of the case. I had some dim idea of eventually editing and collecting some of these pieces for publication in book form, so I had been looking at them on the plane on the way to Wichita. "I have some of the columns here. Would you like me to read one to you?"

She nodded, her eyes wide. But then she frowned and shook her head. "No," she said. "No, I don't want to hear just one of them. I want to hear…all of them."

"Don't be so sure," I said. "The editors at *Bird Watcher's Digest* let me get away with a lot of weird stuff. One column here is actually sort of a spy story. Would you want to hear something like that?"

"Well, of course I would," she said. "If you wrote it. I'm your mother."

THE BIRDER
WHO CAME IN
FROM THE COLD

IN 1985, while I was living in Philadelphia, I met James Bond. No, not that one. The *real* one—James Bond the ornithologist, the author of *Birds of the West Indies.*

This fine gentleman was in his eighties then, and retired from working at the Academy of Natural Sciences, but still willing to talk with anyone about Caribbean ornithology. Although our conversation ranged widely, we said nothing about one singular coincidence of his life: the fact that the British writer Ian Fleming was in Jamaica at the time he was trying to name the hero of his first spy novel. Fleming happened to pick up a copy of *Birds of the West Indies,* and he liked the author's name, and he appropriated it. James Bond the spy, as everyone knows, went on to become one of the best-known characters in modern fiction, while James Bond the ornithologist was stuck with a most unexpected alter ego.

Most people think that this shared name, James Bond, is the main connection between the worlds of bird watching and espionage. However, a much closer link exists. I found out about it quite by accident just a few years ago. Up to now, I have told this story to hardly anyone.

It was a late afternoon in early fall. I was in Holland, a nation of highly educated and cultured people and, of course, many active birders. One of the Dutch experts had found a greater yellowlegs at a pond near the coast, and birders were converging on the scene from all over. I went along; even though I had seen thousands of greater yellowlegs in North America, it seemed intriguing to see one in Europe, where it was such a rare visitor.

At the site there were dozens of birders lined up watching the yellowlegs: lots of Dutch, a few Belgians, even some British and German and Danish and Swedish birders who had driven in to see this one rarity. After I had watched the bird for a while, and discussed its field marks with several people, I noticed one birder coming through the crowd with an alert, nervous air. When he got to me, he stopped. Speaking with a cultured British accent, he addressed me in a strangely stilted way. "It is a rare bird," he said. "But not where you come from."

I sized the man up for a moment. He was dressed a little oddly, with his trench coat buttoned up to his neck and his hat pulled down almost to his eyes, but other than that he seemed normal enough: thin face, sandy hair, quick, darting eyes. I had met enough birders to know that they came in all descriptions. "Yes," I agreed. "Rare in Europe. It's fun to see it here, even if it's a common bird back in the States."

He nodded. "It looks like a juvenile."

"Has to be," I agreed. "Big pale spots on the coverts."

Still speaking in an oddly formal way, he continued. "I saw this species at Jamaica Bay."

"That's a great spot," I said. "Jamaica Bay. All those shorebirds, right in the shadow of New York City."

He nodded again, as if satisfied, and slipped a small package into my hand. "Carlos will meet you at the usual place," he muttered, and turned to leave.

"Wait a sec," I said. "What's this?"

The stranger whipped around. "It's the microfilm, you idiot," he hissed.

"I don't know what you're talking about."

His jaw dropped, and then he looked panicked and perplexed. "But you gave all the right answers! You knew the code!"

"I thought we were just talking about birds. What's going on here, anyway?"

"Not so loud!" the stranger whispered and grabbed the package back. His eyes darted about the crowd. "Wait, let me think. I can't leave here alone if I'm still carrying the microfilm. Come on, come with me." He grasped my arm firmly. Then more loudly, for the sake of bystanders, he said, "There's a pub in the next village. We can have a bite and write up our bird notes for today."

By now I was totally mystified by the man's odd behavior. My curiosity had gotten the best of me, though, so I went along without protest.

At the pub, the stranger seemed to relax a bit. ("You can call me James," he said. "That's not my real name, but you can call me that." Mentally I started to call him Code Name James.) While darkness fell on the quiet village outside the window, we sat and talked about birds. This man obviously loved birding, and he had traveled widely; we spoke of great birding spots that each of us had visited around Europe and North America, and in tropical countries. After Code Name James had had several beers and seemed to be loosened up, I asked him what was going on with the microfilm.

His wary look returned, tempered somewhat by a warm glow from the ale, and he cast a long, suspicious look about the interior of the pub. "I shouldn't tell you. But, well, that's just my job. I'm a secret agent." He saw my look of disbelief and continued. "No, really. Every country has them, you know. But we don't have numbers like oh-oh-seven. My serial number is eight digits long. It's not just a few elite derring-do types saving the world—there are lots of us. And most of the work is pretty boring. I was bored to tears until I got into birding."

I decided to play along. "So you were a spy before you started birding?"

"Yes, actually, I got into birding *because* I was a spy. I was mistaken for a birder."

"How on earth did that happen?"

"It happened in your country," said Code Name James, leaning back and launching into his story. "To the east of Washington, D.C., in Delaware. We had picked a spot on the map for a rendezvous. A little dead-end road —we figured no one would be out there on a road called Port Mahon. I was supposed to meet a double agent there to give him a new high-powered telescope for peering into a certain embassy. So I'm out there, testing this telescope, when a carload of rough-looking characters pulls up. They're all shouting at me: 'Come on! We've found it!' and they grab me and hustle me into their car. I thought I was dead for sure, but the next thing I know, we're down at the edge of a pond looking at this bird, and they tell me it's a white-winged tern."

"Yeah," I interrupted. "I once saw a white-winged tern near the Port Mahon road myself."

Code Name James went on. "And there were all these other birders there, and everyone was having a great time, and then somebody else came roaring up to say they'd found a red-necked stint at Bombay Hook. And we all took off to dash down there! It was so exciting. So, you know, it didn't take long until I was hooked."

"So you were just doing your normal spy stuff and you were mistaken for a birder," I mused. "It used to work the other way. Some of the birders I know in Poland, they used to get picked up by the authorities all the time back in the 1970s, when it was still under the Communist regime. They'd be trying to count migrating hawks along the border, and the police would think they were spies."

"Well, now it's the other way round," said James. "No matter what I'm doing now, with any kind of equipment — telescopes, night scopes, recording gear — people just assume that I'm birding. I was tape-recording the Cuban embassy in London, and everyone figured I was taping the mistle thrush in the park across the street. It's the perfect cover. In fact, I convinced my superiors that all our field operatives should pretend to be birders. So far, my boss hasn't realized how it's going to backfire."

"What? How could it backfire?"

"Well, these blokes aren't just pretending to be birders. They really *are* birders. And you can understand why — being a spy is so bloody boring most of the time. Birding breaks up the monotony. It's unpredictable. It's exciting. It's so much better than the drudgery of secret agent work."

"Okay," I said. "But what does it matter if these spies are birding in their spare time?"

Code Name James gave me a knowing look. "Spare time, indeed. These chaps are not just casual birders. They're in deep. They've got these high-tech wrist radios with satellite linkups, and they're using them to get rare bird alerts. They're figuring out reasons to go do counter-intelligence work on the Texas coast in April, at Point

Pelee in May, in Arizona in July, at Cape May in October. They're concocting stories about security problems along the Amazon and at the national parks in East Africa. Me, I'm about to go infiltrate the Sendero Luminoso movement in Peru."

"I thought the Sendero was pretty much out of business now that what's-his-name is in jail," I protested.

"So what? Think of all the new birds I'll see while I'm trying to confirm that! All those tanagers! All those hummingbirds! Andean condors! Torrent ducks! With birds like that around, who cares if the terrorists aren't active anymore? And speaking of the devil," he said, "look who's here. Kenn, this is Carlos. Carlos, meet Kenn. How are you doing, old chap?"

A swarthy man appeared rather suddenly out of the shadows, sat down at our table, and fixed me with a baleful glare. (I was a little put off by that, but I soon realized that Carlos looked at everyone and everything with a baleful glare.) "Carlos is sort of a celebrity," continued James. "He used to be a shadowy international rogue agent, but now he works with our section. Used to be that his hobby and his profession were in conflict with each other. No more. Now he goes spying and birding, and he's happy as a clam."

He looked a little less happy than the typical clam, I thought, but I decided not to point that out. Carlos nodded at me. "Yah," he said, with a thick accent. "In the past it was very sad. Is sad thing when the passion and the work are so much not good together. I would be going into building to figure out where to plant the hidden microphone, and I would look around and think, This paneling is much too dark for this room! And the carpeting is hideous! They should replace all the draperies and get different style of furniture! And—"

"So," I said, "your passion was—"

"That is right," said Carlos, with a baleful glare. "Interior decorating. That and the stamp collecting, but nobody ever sending me stamps on mail because I was shadowy international agent with no mailing address. Now I give up all that stuff. I am international spy and international birder, with big life list."

"Here," said Code Name James, "feast your eyes on this, Carlos." He reached into his oversized attaché case and pulled out a big telescope. "Brand-new Leica Televid 77. Apochromatic system, fluoride lenses. With this baby, you could read the fine print on a government document from two hundred meters and through two panes of glass."

"Yah," said Carlos, laughing, despite his baleful glare. "Or more likely, from two hundred meters you could count the spots on a spotted sandpiper."

"Sure. But don't tell my boss that. He thinks I needed this scope for my *work*." They both laughed uproariously. "Oh, I got this new Sennheiser directional mike, too. Great for recording bird voices in the forest, but I told them I needed it for recording conversations in crowded rooms. And wait till you see the vehicle I requested!

Four-wheel drive, sunroof, window mounts for the scopes, and —" He glanced out the window at the parking lot, and broke off in midsentence.

Outside, a beautiful woman was stepping out of a little red convertible. As we watched, she walked into the pub and stood looking anxiously around.

We all stared. Even Carlos's glare seemed a little less baleful. The woman was stunning, a classic beauty, with dark hair and deep, flashing eyes. In a film, her part would have been played by a young Lena Olin. But I had only a moment to think about that. As soon as she saw us, she came straight over to our table. "Good," she breathed. "I was hoping I might find you here."

So there's some truth to it after all, I thought. *The gorgeous women in the spy movies — they really do exist, and they really do hang around with these trench coat guys.* Then I glanced at my companions and was startled to realize that they didn't recognize her any more than I did. But by now the woman was sitting down at our table and leaning close. "I need your help," she said softly.

James found his voice first. "Um, yes, miss, what makes you think we can help you?"

"I know what you do," she said. Her eyes strayed down to James's oversized attaché case, which was still standing open, revealing high-powered binoculars and telescopes and recording equipment, all his spy gear. *We're done for now,* I told myself, *if this babe is a spy for some enemy power. She's recognized all the paraphernalia. She knows these guys are spies, and she'll think that I'm one, too*. But the woman had more to say. "I'm sure one of you can help me." She looked around and took a deep breath before continuing. "I'm almost certain I heard a Tengmalm's owl in a wood lot near here, but I've never heard one before, and I need someone to confirm it. There's only room in my car for one more person. Can one of you come with me?"

"Why do you think we can help you identify an owl?"

"Well," she said, gesturing at the pile of espionage equipment, "you're obviously birders."

"And *you* are a birder?" I asked.

"Of course!" She laughed and gave me a condescending look. "What do you think I am? A secret agent or something?"

The last we saw of Code Name James, he was waving to us with a rather goofy expression on his face as he rode away with the beautiful woman in her little red convertible. Watching them go, I was left wondering: Was she really a birder, or was that just a clever ruse by a counterspy? Was he really a spy, or was that just a good yarn? Would they find the Tengmalm's owl? Would she find out what his real name was?

I never learned the answers, because I never saw them again. So that's all there is to the story. Now you know as much about it as I do. But now that you've heard the story, I'll have to ask you not to remember it.

Seriously. This is a matter of national security. If you repeat any of this, you may find strange characters in trench coats lurking under your bed or behind the door. Worse yet, the American Birding Association may deny any knowledge of your activities. So you're much better off just to forget every word of this.

Got that? Good. This storyteller will self-destruct in twenty seconds. Have a nice day.

Parking Lot Birds

A FRIEND OF MINE recently went off to study birds in the Caatinga, an arid and thorny region of northeastern Brazil. He told me it was a habitat that had been neglected by biologists. His project struck me as a worthy one, of course, but I pointed out to him that there was another important bird habitat, much closer to home, that the biologists had overlooked at least as much: parking lots.

I don't know why this habitat should have been so universally ignored by ornithologists. To be sure, it is not an endangered habitat at the moment; the total acreage of parking lots in North America is probably still increasing. So a study of parking lots would not get any funding from the bird conservation groups. Not yet, anyway.

But what about the future? Some day soon (as any science fiction fan knows), we'll be able to beam ourselves from place to place. At the push of a button, we will transform ourselves into electrical pulses and then transmit ourselves to another spot. (It's just one step of technology beyond the current fax machine. Already we can fax pieces of paper from place to place, and all we have to do is apply that science to living things — in other words, learn about The Fax of Life.) When that happens, people may not bother with cars anymore, except as status symbols. Why sit in traffic when you can just beam yourself home from work? With fewer cars, there will be less reason for parking lots, and those old asphalt slabs may be plowed up and turned into forests. What will happen then to the birds that live in parking lots? We should start studying the problem now, before it turns into an emergency.

Parking lots near the beach, the kind that are thronged with cars in summer, are not really deserted in the off-season. After the human crowds depart, crowds of gulls often move in, to rest on these broad open expanses.

This is not just a phenomenon of the coast. Gulls foraging along the Mississippi in winter will leave the river to rest in parking lots in St. Louis. Gulls from southern Lake Michigan will fly several miles into Indiana to rest on the parking lots of Notre Dame. There are even parking lots in far-inland places like Oklahoma and Utah that are favored by gulls at times.

To anyone who knows how raucous gulls can be when they're feeding, the peaceful air of these resting flocks may come as a surprise. Bills pointing into the breeze, the gulls line up all facing the same direction. The flocks have an orderly pattern, as if they were subconsciously heeding the regular rows of painted white or yellow stripes that mark off the slots for cars. Ruffling their feathers, standing on one leg, preening, dozing, the gulls while away the hours.

Of course, they will not rest for long. When the tide changes, or when the shift changes at the local garbage dump, or when some other kind of feeding opportunity presents itself, they will be off in a blizzard of wings. But for the moment, they are quiet. They are, in a sense, parked.

Naturally, gulls are not the only birds to occur in this unnatural habitat. Some songbird types are found there as well. Along the Pacific Coast, but only there, one species wins the prize as the prevailing small bird in parking lots: Brewer's blackbird.

Incidentally, the name requires a bit of interpretation. This species was named after a particular person— Thomas Brewer, a nineteenth-century Boston physician and ornithologist—and not just after some guy who ran a brewery. I bring up this point only because someone once asked me if "brewer's blackbirds" liked to drink beer. No, they don't. They're not hanging around in the parking lot waiting for more suds from the brewery; they're waiting for tortilla chips and bagel crumbs.

That's one of the things that makes parking lot birding effective. While some birds, such as gulls, seem to regard these big expanses of concrete as no more than good places to rest, other birds come here for the feeding opportunities. And of course the opportunities vary with location. At least away from prime territory for resting gulls, for a site to be classified as an IBPL (Important Bird Parking Lot), it should be near a food source. The parking lot for a fast-food joint inevitably will offer better birding than the parking lot for a fabric store.

At any rate, whenever I visit the California coast, I'm always struck by the fact that Brewer's blackbirds are everywhere in the parking lots and on the sidewalks around shops and restaurants. The males, sharp, glossy blue-black birds with staring pale eyes, and the females, softer gray with brown eyes, go stepping about among the cars and pedestrians, seeking crumbs left behind by the shoppers. It's impressive to see how unconcerned they are about the bustle of human activity. But another thing that impresses me is that Brewer's blackbirds are *not* major parking lot birds elsewhere. Although the species is widespread over the western two-thirds of the continent, I have not seen it dominating the parking lot scene anywhere except along the coast.

It may be that, in other areas, Brewer's blackbirds are edged out of this prime habitat by other species. In Tucson, Arizona, where I lived for several years, it is the great-tailed grackle that reigns as the king of the parking lots. These grackles are big birds: the males can be a foot and a half long if we count the tail, and we might as well.

When they are flying, they look as if they might be dragged down out of the air by their long, heavy tails. Around parking lots, though, the great-tailed grackles spend more time walking than flying, and more time standing around than walking. While the males are loafing at the edges of the lot, they often give voice to a bizarre series of noises — creaking, grating, crashing, scraping noises, along with factory whistles and clicks and clanks. They have a mechanical sound, as if the birds might feel right at home among all the motorized vehicles in the parking lots.

Great-tailed grackles normally have pale yellow eyes after they grow up. A few years ago, however, idly studying the grackles around a burger joint in Tucson, I noticed that a couple of them — apparently adults — had dark eyes and some missing feathers. This touched off my curiosity. In the time since, visiting the parking lots of numerous fast-food restaurants, I have continued to see odd things in the appearance of various grackles. Some have the wrong eye color; some are missing most of the feathers on their heads; some have patches of white, or generally dull plumage. Many of these anomalies could have been caused by deficiencies in the diets of these birds. If you're sitting in the parking lot eating your lunch and notice that you're surrounded by scruffy and malnourished grackles, it could be enough to make you look at your McFrench fries in a whole new light.

Not all birds seem to be affected in a bad way by eating

human junk food. A few have been with us long enough to adapt, to thrive on such fare. The everyday house sparrow has been a satellite of human civilization for probably more than two thousand years, adapting to life around city-states of the Mediterranean region, following the Roman legions as they marched across Europe, and later hitching rides with colonists who went to other continents. In some ways, house sparrows are the perfect parking lot birds. They get along okay on the worst food that we can dish out, and they are resourceful at finding their own food in parking lots as well.

Have you ever noticed that, when you're driving, the front end of your car may develop a collection of smashed dead insects? Well, the house sparrows have noticed that, too. Many times I've seen house sparrows fluttering around in front of parked cars, picking choice morsels from the still-warm radiators. Not only does the car help to gather up insects for these birds but the hot engine cooks them, too: baked beetles, roasted roaches, fried flies, and other delicacies.

House sparrows are not the only birds to take advantage of these meals on wheels. In desert regions, cactus wrens often do the same thing. Cactus wrens are just as inquisitive as other wrens, but they seem much less nervous than their relatives about coming out in the open. (Come to think of it, since they live in the desert, they're out in the open most of the time.) At various parks and recreation areas in the American Southwest, you can find cactus wrens working the parking lots, collecting their own entrance fees in the form of grilled insects.

If you come back to your car in the parking lot and find one of these little birds picking bugs off the radiator, you may say something like "Oh, how cute." But your reaction might be different—you might say things that would not be repeatable in polite company—if you happened to be in New Zealand, and the bird picking things off your car were that parrot called the kea.

The kea is a very large and bulky parrot, the color of muddy moss but with a flash of flame red under the wings. Its bill has a very long, curved, pointed upper mandible, a feature that Captain Hook would have envied. And the kea makes full use of this bill.

I've heard it said that owning a normal pet parrot is like having a two-year-old child with a can opener on its face. If that is so, then a flock of wild keas is like a gang of teenagers with chain saws on their faces. There is still some debate, in the high pastures of the South Island, about whether keas actually kill sheep. Whether or not they do, there's no doubt that keas are very good at taking the sheep apart once they're dead. And keas are good at taking other things apart as well.

Once, while visiting a little-used parking lot at high elevation in the Fiordland area of southern New Zealand, I noticed a family who had just come back to find that their car had been vandalized. The windshield wipers were bent askew, with the softer parts ripped away, and most of the rubber molding had been pulled from the edges of the windows. After assessing the damage, and cursing the likely culprits, the head of the family climbed into the car and slammed the door — and the windshield fell out onto the hood. With the glass tossed into the trunk, the family drove away, curses still emanating from the driver's seat. Meanwhile, down at the far end of the parking lot, three keas were studiously working on another car.

The kea may be just getting revenge for the fact that it has one of the shortest official bird names in the world. All the same, considering how many Americans are in love with their cars, it's probably just as well that we don't have any keas on this continent.

It may be that the easiest parking lot birds to get along with are those that simply rest there, like the gulls, rather than trying to garner anything edible from the cars or from the littering humans. But I want to end by mentioning another kind of bird associated with parking lots, living above the lots, not on them.

Some kinds of parking lots are well lighted at night. Perhaps meant to deter thugs, the lights attract bugs; many kinds of moths and beetles, and a host of other insects, will fly to the lights. This in itself is reason enough for a closet entomologist like me to stop and check these lighted lots at night. But the insects, in turn, attract certain birds. Nighthawks, which feed on insects that they capture in graceful flight, are regular nighttime visitors to the airspace above these lighted areas. Many times, while out for walks at night, I have paused to watch the graceful aerial ballet of nighthawks high above well-lit parking lots.

Once while driving across Venezuela, I arrived after dark at a hotel in the middle of a town in arid country. The parking area was a large lot behind the hotel, fenced in and brightly lit for protection, so I maneuvered the car into one of the few remaining spaces with the shouted aid of the young attendant. As I was turning to go inside, I noticed several lesser nighthawks foraging quietly overhead.

Unlike the common nighthawk, with its frequent buzzy *peent* calls, the lesser nighthawk is typically a silent bird. The dozen or so that were now overhead were flying in total silence, coursing back and forth with slow, buoyant wingbeats, seeming to float above the lights.

The parking lot attendant came up to see what was wrong, but when he saw that I was staring upward, he relaxed. With an angelic smile, he explained to me in Spanish: "Swallows," he said, pointing at the nighthawks. "It is a luxury of the hotel."

Right you are, I thought. Who cares what the bird is called, swallow or nighthawk or something else? The young man was right: we should consider it a luxury that there are still birds that live around the edges of our cities and built-up places, and even in — or above — our parking lots.

"IT WAS IN A PARKING LOT, wasn't it," my mother asked, "where you found that baby bird? That first one that you brought into the house?"

"Yeah, it was," I said, ruefully. "Yeah, I'd forgotten about that."

"I'll never forget it," she said, smiling, her face taking on a faraway look. "You seemed so..." She paused, searching for the right word. "You looked so *nonchalant.* Such an expression of...misplaced savoir-faire. Strolling through the house, toward your room, so casual, with a lump inside your shirt that was going *'cheep cheep cheep cheep'*...and you were whistling, too, as if you thought you could drown it out."

"Okay, okay," I said. "I must have been, what, seven years old? It was while we were still in Indiana."

"And you looked so *surprised* when your father asked you about it. Such a wide-eyed, innocent look. 'Who, *me?* Oh, you mean *that* bird sound! I was just about to *tell* you about that!' But you looked so adorable that we couldn't get mad."

"Hmmmh. Thanks a lot. Adorableness is what I've always aspired to."

"You always had it," Mom said. "Lucky for you, too. Considering all the times that you deserved to be in trouble."

"What's that saying about little kids? God made them cute so we wouldn't kill them? Cuteness was the problem, though, in that case." I had found this gawky, pinfeathered baby bird in the corner of a parking lot on the way home from school and had jumped to the conclusion that it must have been abandoned by its parents. The parent birds undoubtedly were watching from somewhere nearby, and the fledgling probably would have been fine if I had left it alone. But I was convinced that this hapless, helpless creature needed urgent care. Besides, I had the idea that it might grow up to be some rare kind of bird that I had never seen before. So I had scooped it up and brought it home.

My attempt to smuggle this waif into my room had failed, of course, so Mom had set it up in a box in the kitchen. Announcing self-importantly that I had been studying birds and that I knew how to feed them, I went out in the yard to try to catch some insects.

At first I had no success at feeding the new adoptee. I had caught a large grasshopper and a couple of beetles, and I could not persuade the bird to even try to eat them. My mother watched the proceedings for a while and then gently suggested an alternate approach, taking bits of hamburger and molding them into tiny pellets of protein, then offering them with a pair of tweezers. I have no idea where she got this idea, but I recall vividly that it worked:

the bird opened its mouth wide and proceeded to swallow prodigious amounts of food.

For the next couple of days the bird was chowing down on hamburger with gusto and begging for more, looking more alert, its feathers continuing to grow out. But on the third day I insisted on taking over the menu planning again. The bird had to learn to eat normal foods, I said, or it would be unprepared for life in the wild. We couldn't have the bird out on its own, searching the neighborhood in vain for bits of hamburger (or, as my brother suggested, flying out to the country and attacking cows). So I put it back on the insect diet. That afternoon I got it to eat a couple of flies and a few pieces of earthworm, but these natural foods didn't seem to go down as well.

Early on the morning of the fourth day I got up to find the bird lying lifeless in its box in the kitchen. My mother tried to soften the blow, saying that perhaps there was nothing I could have done, perhaps it had already suffered internal injuries before I had found it. She said, too, that young birds faced many dangers and that many would fail to survive in the wild. Although I didn't know it at the time, I had just taken part in a scenario that is played out countless times every year, with countless baby birds killed by the well-meaning humans who "adopt" them. But I doubt that it would have been any consolation to me then to have put the plight of this individual into a larger context. I was still too young to accept the idea that stories might not have happy endings, that good intentions in themselves might not be enough.

FREEDOM
FOR SALE

THEY WERE BARRED PARAKEETS, all right. A pair of them. Henry West had found them half an hour earlier and had come back to tell us; now we all stood and stared. The parakeets stared back...from behind bars, from their cage in the crowded marketplace in the Mexican mountain town of Teziutlán.

I was amazed. These tiny green parrots are hard to come by in Mexico. Even as far south as the Guatemalan border, in the cloud forests of Lagos de Montebello, the best that we can hope for is a flyover. On several trips there I had heard them calling on the side road to Cinco Lagos, and I had called out, "Barred parakeets!" — leaving my tour groups disappointed to see nothing more than a flock high overhead, small, stubby birds making shrill cries, looking black against the sky. I had to go to South America before I ever saw a barred parakeet perched. And only once had I seen a small flock as far north as Teziutlán. Could these possibly be local birds?

The bird vendor stood nearby, dignified but a little self-conscious under all this foreign attention. Yes, he said, all of his birds had been captured quite near Teziutlán; he made a sweeping gesture to take in all the birds in the other cages, a ragtag collection of orioles, robins, buntings, brown-backed solitaires, and the like. And he had caught them all himself. When I asked how he captured them, his eyes narrowed — did he think I was going to steal his trade secrets? — and he answered shortly that they had been baited with corn. Orioles and solitaires would not come to corn bait, I knew, even if parakeets would, so I dismissed that answer as being the best that I would get, but then I noticed another important difference between these parakeets and the other cage birds. I looked more closely. "You must have caught these *pericos* very recently," I said, in my best nonchalant Spanish.

At this the man beamed broadly. Yes, he said, very recently indeed. Yesterday! They were his newest birds.

I translated his answer for the people in my tour group, and we all contemplated the obvious truth of what he said. It was clear: the parakeets had to be recent captives, because they were still in beautiful condition. They were not yet half bald and scaly and slow from the poor diet, their feathers were not yet ragged and frayed, their wings and tails not yet worn down to stubs from abrasion in the cramped cage. But all of these changes would come to pass for the parakeets, soon, inevitably. As they had for all the birds in the other cages.

No one said it, but we could feel that everyone was thinking the same thing; and I knew I should dissuade my companions. So I told them that we should not buy those birds, not even to purchase their freedom and release them to the wild. If we did, other birds would suffer for it.

Of course, the problem had many dimensions. This bird vendor had his family to feed: two wide-eyed moppets who stared at us from behind another stack of cages, maybe more kids at home. And yes, of course, I cared about the children as well as the birds. But if the man could not sell his birds, perhaps he would turn to some other profession. If the birds sold quickly, he would go out and trap some more. How much pressure could the barred parakeet population stand, here at its northern limit? Probably not much; it was up to us, the consumers, to exercise restraint. Boycott was our only weapon.

I guess it was a fine little speech that I made. Everyone seemed to be convinced.

Except me.

I was thinking about the barred parakeets for the rest of the afternoon. I thought of how the cloud forest must look from their perspective. Each gigantic tree here would be a world in itself, with every great limb coated with moss, hung with vines, festooned with odd epiphytic plants that never touch soil. A tiny parakeet could spend the whole day exploring just one of these trees. Or it could leap up and fly, in a shrill flock with others of its kind, out over the valleys and ridges below Teziutlán. When the evening fog shrouded the forest in mystery, or when the morning sun sparkled on a billion drops of water in the trees, the barred parakeets would always be at home in the cloud forest.

Then I thought about their capture, the crude trap dropping, their world reduced to a rough cage ten inches square. And my "sermon" about boycotting the bird trade seemed empty and pointless when I considered these individual birds and their future in that cage. We were not facing a big international trade in wildlife here — just Ernesto Sánchez, an honest man trying to make a living in Teziutlán. What we did here would not make any difference. Except to those two barred parakeets.

That evening, while my companions tucked into their second round of enchiladas and beer, I slipped out of the cantina and returned to the market. The bird vendor was packing up to leave, but when he saw me coming he knew he had a sale.

The asking price for the pair of parakeets worked out to about fifteen dollars. *You poor devil,* I thought, *do you have any idea what you could get for these birds in the States?* Better not to tell him that. Better not to think about it. I haggled the price down to about fourteen dollars, with the cage thrown in. They're not very valuable birds, amigo; don't bother to trap any more of them.

The members of my tour group, bless them, didn't give me even half as much grief as I deserved for contradicting myself. "We knew that you were going to go back and buy the birds yourself," someone told me. "We decided that this afternoon. It was obvious from the way you were talking about it." Maybe they were right; I couldn't argue.

The next morning at the edge of the cloud forest we held our own little release-of-the-hostages ceremony. Henry, the experienced bird bander, deftly pulled one bird from the cage to hold up for photographs. The outraged parakeet shrieked and gnawed on Henry's knuckle, drawing a drop of blood, while the cameras clicked. Then — careful of the timing, now, we wanted to release them together — I let the second bird out of the cage as Henry launched the first.

Would it make a good story to claim that they seemed grateful? Actually, they streaked away into the forest together and disappeared immediately. But we were not looking for any show of sentiment. The parakeets had their freedom again, and, we told each other, it was just as important that the forest had its parakeets again. With the uneasy sense that comes from following one's heart instead of one's head, we crossed our fingers and hoped that the birds would not be caught a second time, that our good intentions would not have helped to pave the road to oblivion.

Into Thin Air

THINK ABOUT IT: Air is a fluid, like water. It has weight; given the chance, it tends to flow downhill.

There is always plenty of air hugging the surface of this planet, down low, within a few thousand feet of sea level, down where most of us live. There is less of it at higher elevations in the mountains. At the highest levels, the air is extremely thin, and it seems cold and anemic and ineffective, too, as if this air were somehow too gutless and weak to fight its way down to the more desirable lower elevations.

Strange ideas, I know. But when you breathe such thin air, your mind may do odd things like that. I experienced that for myself a few years ago, when I spent several days in the high Andes of Peru with the Danish ornithologist, Niels Krabbe, looking for rare birds.

I had run into Niels quite by chance. In the fog-drenched forest of the Carpish Tunnel area in the highlands of central Peru, some friends and I had noticed a slight gap in the roadside vegetation that led to a faint, narrow trail into the deep woods. We were walking down this trail and congratulating ourselves on being true explorers when we encountered — of all things — a mist net. Aluminum poles, precise nylon mesh, a very modern device for capturing birds. Edging around it and continuing down the trail, we encountered a second mist net, and then a third. And in the clearing beyond that one, a bespectacled Dane was carefully photographing the small flycatcher he had just removed from the net.

Niels had planned to leave here soon, to ride the slow buses back to Peru's capital city of Lima. I was planning to drop off my friends at the airport at Tingo Maria — this was in the days before the Sendero guerrillas took over that region, when gringos could still go to Tingo in safety — and I had a four-wheel-drive truck that had to be taken back to Lima, where it had been rented. It seemed logical that we should join forces. Between Tingo Maria and Lima towered the ridge of the Andes, forcing the road to over fifteen thousand feet. That, however, was not an obstacle. That was an opportunity. The road would take us to look for the birds that lived in high places.

Foremost on our list of wanted birds was the white-bellied cinclodes, a rare species that had posed a mystery for years. It had been known from some old museum specimens from scattered vague points in the Andes, but until recently there had been no exact localities pinpointed, no stakeouts where one could reasonably hope to see this bird.

It was no trick to see some other kinds of cinclodes. The bar-winged cinclodes, for example, was among the most familiar birds of the upper Andes. A thrush-sized brown bird with a stodgy, solid-citizen look, it was always walking around in gravelly spots, always flying up from the roadsides in the mountains. Another, the white-winged cinclodes, was not hard to find around mountain streams. But the white-bellied one, *Cinclodes palliatus,* had eluded practically all birders and ornithologists — until very recently. Niels and I had both heard news of the discovery of a high-elevation bog that harbored this ultra-rare bird. Armed with the directions, we were eager to visit the site.

Leaving Tingo Maria, passing through the valley at Huánuco, we headed up into the mountains. We made a stop to find the scarce brown-flanked tanager, and looked at spinetails and chat-tyrants in the stunted stands of gnarly *Polylepis* trees. Driving higher, out onto the open, dry grassland of the puna, we stopped to look at the occasional aplomado falcon and to study the flocks of cryptic gray ground-tyrants. Then we went higher still. On the fifteenth of August, we went beyond the high pass at Ticlio and up the Marcapomacocha road, somewhere around fifteen thousand feet above sea level, and arrived at our main destination.

We knew, consulting our crude map, that we had come to the right place. We had passed the abandoned roadside chapel, turned off on the neglected side track, come to the deserted sheds at the edge of the dropoff. Everything had an eerie, empty look. Nothing moved except the wind in the dry puna grass, and much of the land was barren even of grass: jagged peaks of bare rock, slopes of gray and orange gravel. Across from us, on the face of an immense peak, sunlight glared on permanent snowfields. There was no haze or dust in the thin, clear air, and everything stood out with a startling clarity. It was a spectacular scene — but we had been surrounded by spectacular scenes for days now, dazzled by dizzying vistas in this land of too much light and too little air. Now we just squinted and looked down.

A rough track led down the steep hillside from where we stood. It might have been a road once, but our directions said we should park where we were and walk down. Far below us, several hundred feet down, lay a wide, boggy depression where the rare cinclodes was supposed to live.

Niels Krabbe is tough as nails, and rumor has it that he has done outlandish things in his pursuit of birds around the world. But he is not altogether lacking in common sense. Now, studying the long drop to the bog below us, he observed, "We will be exhausting ourselves if we must climb back up the mountain at this elevation." I had to agree; in this thin atmosphere, even walking on level ground was tiring. Niels turned to look at me. "Your truck, it has the four-wheel drive, yes? I think we can drive down to the bog."

Sure, I thought, *you* don't have to pay for the damage. But our vehicle — a Russian-made version of a Land

Rover — had performed well so far. And there was a certain international flair to the idea of an American and a Dane wrecking a Russian truck on a Peruvian mountain. By hugging the uphill side of the track, and reversing a few times on switchbacks, I was able to drive all the way down the slope.

The bog that now stretched away at our level was quite large — at least a few acres in extent. Splitting up to search it more effectively, we headed out walking in two directions. It was slow going. There was little standing water, but the ground seemed permanently saturated: soft underfoot, slippery and muddy in the narrow spaces between the irregular hummocks of grass.

As I picked my way across the bog, stopping occasionally for a few deep breaths, I was musing on this strange habitat and on the strange idea that the white-bellied cinclodes should be living here. This whole region of the high Andes was dominated by very dry puna grassland, but here and there were scattered bogs like this: depressions that held the infrequent rain, flat areas fed by runoff from glaciers. We had passed several bogs that had looked not too different from this one. Why should the rarest cinclodes choose this particular spot? Were the rumors of its discovery really true?

But before I had time to get bogged down in pessimistic thoughts, I was spun around by a shout of "*Palliatus!* I see the *Cinclodes palliatus!*" Niels, who speaks several languages, reverts to the scientific names of birds when he's excited; fortunately, he doesn't revert to Danish. "Come quickly! It is over here!"

There was no need for directions. The bird was out in the open, dashing across a low spot, pausing boldly atop a hummock to look back at us. One glance was enough to confirm that this was no bar-winged cinclodes: it looked half again as large, and its underparts were brilliant snowy white from chin to tail. Without a doubt, this was the white-bellied cinclodes, one of the least-known birds of the high Andes.

Stumbling across the bog toward the cinclodes, we realized that there was a second one not far away. The two birds were evidently a mated pair; they stayed more or less together, moving ahead of us each time we attempted to approach. We soon decided that it was better to keep our distance and watch them through binoculars and telescope. Their behavior reminded me of North American mockingbirds: they would run across the ground and then pause, cocking their tails up over their backs. When one of the cinclodes was hunting for food, it would stare straight down at the ground and then probe at the soil with its heavy bill. Always the birds kept one wary eye on us, the intruders in their highland world.

Big, boldly patterned, rich chestnut above contrasting with bright white below, these white-bellied cinclodes looked much more striking and elegant than the common bar-winged cinclodes. I commented on this to Niels, and he nodded, but then he murmured, "The bird is elegant partly because we know it is very rare, yes?" And I could not disagree.

At length the two cinclodes got away from us when we detoured around a low, wet area, and then we discovered a second pair of them. Just as wary as the first pair, they kept well away from us, running rapidly over the damp ground. We never saw them fly. We speculated that these rare birds might spend their whole lives here, never wandering from this isolated bog.

While we were watching this second pair, a puna hawk came sailing over, and moments later an uproar broke out on the nearby slope. A flock of at least seventy stout, short-tailed birds burst from the ground and went rocketing overhead, calling in discordant alarm. These were birds I had never seen before, but I recognized them as rufous-bellied seedsnipes—members of a bizarre South American family, unlike anything else in the world. They were certainly not the least bit like ordinary snipes. I had seen other types of seedsnipes elsewhere in Peru, but this, the largest species, was known only from the highest elevations.

Another flock of rufous-bellied seedsnipes came up from the far ridge, and for the next half hour we kept seeing and hearing these strange creatures. Noisy regiments would hurtle by in a high, bounding flight, swinging away wide past the gray slopes and distant peaks, sweeping back past us. They looked unearthly. Their hoarse, scraping calls, echoing over the slopes, would have made an appropriate sound on Mars — or on any other planet where the air was thin.

But the strangest sensation came when I heard, in this alien landscape, a sound that was utterly familiar.

It came from behind me, and even as I was turning to look, I knew what I would see: a little flock of Baird's sandpipers, calling in flight, circling in to alight at the edge of a rivulet in the bog. This was a voice that I knew well. I had learned it as a boy in Kansas, when the sandpipers passed through on their long migrations, and I had heard it many times since from migrating birds during spring and fall. I had heard it in summer on the high Arctic tundra, the only area of the globe where this bird nested and raised its young. Now I was hearing it in the last of the three worlds of the Baird's sandpiper — below the Equator, above the tree line, on the South American puna, where it would wait out the season of the northern winter.

Instinctively I raised my binoculars to look at the little group of sandpipers as they settled on the wet margin, stretched their wings, fluttered a bit, and began to preen or pick at the mud. There were seven of them. Six were adults, but one was clearly a juvenile bird, with crisp white scalloping on the back and wings.

Wait a minute, I said to myself, *this is only the fifteenth of August. What is that bird doing here?*

With a growing sense of disbelief, I began to calculate the dates. In far northern Canada and Alaska, where the

Baird's sandpiper nested, it did not even arrive before the last days of May. Even if it laid its eggs right away — figure three weeks' incubation time for the average small sandpiper — this young bird could not have hatched any more than seven or eight weeks ago, probably less. And here it was a continent and a half away, feeding placidly at the edge of a high Andean marsh. Fifty days old, it had already flown six thousand miles from its birthplace.

And this infant bird had flown not only far, but *high*. A bird that came in by air among these dizzying peaks had to be flying even higher than where we now stood, those small wings beating, that small heart pumping, up where the air was so thin . . .

The very thought made me gasp for breath. The idea of flying above these heights, above this towering horizon that now seemed to be turning and tilting crazily around me . . . I had to sit down to think about this. All my energy seemed to have vanished into the thin air. Glad for an excuse to rest, I collapsed on the ground, looking around at this stark and beautiful land and seeing it in a new light.

This landscape is not alien, I told myself, *but you are.* After all, the birds were right at home: rare cinclodes that never moved from this remote bog; bizarre seedsnipes that roamed the highest ridges; baby sandpipers that flew halfway around the world to be here. Rare birds all, in their own ways, they all belonged here. It was only we, the watchers, who were out of place.

Spring on the Central Highway

A CHILD WHO GROWS UP next to a major highway might be forgiven for developing an incurable case of wanderlust. The early influence of seeing all those travelers passing through, bound for exotic destinations, might well excite the child's imagination, sparking curiosity about distant lands and a desire to emulate the adventures of the travelers. Such was my experience as a boy in Kansas. One of the earth's great corridors of travel essentially passed through my backyard; and although this invisible highway was utterly unknown to most people, it had a profound influence on my view of the world.

Most people, in fact, would be doubly confused at the suggestion that Kansas would lie on a major migration route for shorebirds. The term "shorebirds" itself could be taken to suggest any bird of the water's edge, any gull or tern or heron, perhaps, and the uninitiated would expect such birds to be prevalent at the seashore, far from an interior state like Kansas. But in bird watcher parlance, "shorebirds" are members of a few specific families of birds, primarily sandpipers and plovers. Many of those might more accurately have been called "tundra birds," as they nest on tundra of the Far North, raising their young amid the abundance of insect life and other food during the brief Arctic summer. Those birds might be on their nesting range for only a couple of months out of the year, leaving as soon as their young are independent. Flying south again, those sandpipers and plovers will forage along the water's edge wherever they can find it: not just on coastal estuaries but on lakeshores, river bars, marshes, flooded fields. They define "shore" much more generously than we would.

Among the shorebirds of the Americas, there are a few that stand out as extreme long-distance migrants. I started getting to know those birds when I was a boy of eleven or twelve, exploring the areas I could reach by bicycle from my parents' house in Wichita. For all the birds that I could not find within my limited radius, it seemed I found inordinate numbers of shorebirds. On the muddy margins of the little sandpit ponds, on the temporary mud flats along the river, flocks of shorebirds showed up all spring and throughout the long fall season. Rare ones, too, or at least species that the books suggested were rare. For example, the softly patterned little Baird's sandpipers — the same birds that would thrill me, years later, when I saw them high in the Andes — were described in my books as decidedly scarce, but I saw them in numbers. The big chestnut-colored sandpipers called Hudsonian godwits were regular visitors in spring, even though Roger Tory Peterson had written that they were rare birds. White-rumped sandpipers, American golden-plovers, buff-breasted sandpipers, all appeared in spring within a few miles of my parents' house.

Gradually, as I explored and read and learned more, I realized what was happening. These were the shorebirds that traveled the farthest, nesting above the Arctic Circle and wintering in southernmost South America. In spring they were arrowing north through the center of the North American continent, perhaps pausing along the Texas coast and then moving up through Oklahoma and Kansas and Nebraska and the Dakotas and the Prairie Provinces of Canada, then making a final leap over the boreal forest to the open tundra at the top of the world. The Great Plains, lying between the Rockies and the forested East, form a natural corridor for these great travelers. Avid bird watchers on the Atlantic or Pacific coasts could hardly hope to see a Baird's sandpiper in spring, but I could expect to see flocks of them on the mud flats at Dolese's Sand & Gravel or even on the grassy field behind South High School.

Growing up next to this major travel route, I was influenced by the sense that great journeys are possible, even inevitable. I dreamed of following the shorebirds to the Arctic, to the tropics, to distant shores. Unfortunately, my focus on the exotic and the distant came at the expense of my appreciation for the here and now. This immense highway in the sky brought wonderful birds within reach, but I didn't see it as a reason to stay there; I saw it as an inspiration to get out of Kansas, to follow the example of these migrants.

So I did. From the time I was sixteen, I was away most of the time, traveling all over North America and then farther afield. I thought I knew Kansas birds well enough that I wouldn't need to think about them anymore. Not until I had been away for years did I begin to fully appreciate the remarkable spring migration of the shorebirds through the Great Plains—the phenomenon that had been so near at hand when I was growing up, and that I had so easily taken for granted.

And even more years passed before I made a point of going back to experience it again. My boyhood birding pal, Jeff Cox, was now J. A. Cox, Ph.D., and living in another state, but he was still as skilled and enthusiastic as ever in pursuit of birds. In late May one year, we got together in Wichita and headed out to the wildlife refuges northwest of the city.

I had forgotten the sense of sheer abundance of birds on the prairies in spring. Over the fields were clouds of Franklin's gulls, smartly patterned small gulls that wintered on the coast of Peru and were now migrating to the marshes of the Dakotas. Meadowlarks sang from the fence posts along the roads, western kingbirds perched on the wires, red-winged blackbirds flashed their scarlet epaulets from cattails in the roadside ditches. Best of all, the shorebirds were everywhere. Big, colorful Hudsonian godwits were there, wading in the shallows, and little parties of Wilson's phalaropes. Stilt sandpipers and Baird's sandpipers were present by the hundreds, white-rumped sandpipers and semipalmated sandpipers by the thousands, with lesser numbers of more than a dozen other kinds of sandpipers and plovers. Wherever we came to the water's edge, the mud flats teemed with life.

Most of the shorebirds we saw that day were heading for the Arctic, and were still at least fifteen hundred miles from their destinations. But in spring these northbound shorebirds have an air of urgency, an intensity that is missing when they drift back south a few months later. We could feel their restlessness. They foraged nervously, chattering and shifting about constantly. Flocks would suddenly spring up, sweep wide over the surrounding country before returning to settle on the flats, only to be off again moments later.

Jeff and I were driving a back road between two refuges when we spotted a small flock of American golden-plovers in the air, and we jumped out of the car to watch them. They circled once and then came in to land at the back of a large plowed field, reminding us of what we already knew: these most beautiful of the shorebirds were not tied to the shore. Wintering on the grassy pampas of Argentina, nesting on relatively high and dry regions of Arctic tundra, they had only a casual use for shorelines during their long migrations.

As we were hauling out our telescopes to look at the distant flock, we saw more golden-plovers flying. Swift in the air, they swept past us like living torpedoes, streamlined and powerful. We watched as they dwindled in the distance, but then they turned, they were coming back, more than a score of beautiful golden-plovers headed right for us, pitching in to land barely twenty yards away from where we stood.

Instinctively we froze, and the birds did, too, eyeing us warily. We could see every detail: the golden spangles of the back, the velvety black of the breast, the white stripe that traced the trim neck of each bird. Elegant and sleek, they were marvels of natural design, small birds that weighed only a few ounces and yet had the strength to make this great journey that spanned continents. They were motionless now, but not at rest: still only as an arrow is still when the archer has drawn back the bow to its fullest reach. As soon as they were released, they would be vaulting toward the horizon — just as I had, years before, when I left my boyhood home to travel, to follow birds like these.

MY PARENTS were strong and courageous people, but I didn't fully understand or appreciate that when I was growing up. One of the bravest things that they ever had to do, as I came to understand much later, was watch me leave home at the age of sixteen.

By that time I was totally consumed with curiosity about birds and feeling driven to travel. I knew that there were hundreds of different species of birds in North America that I was unlikely ever to see in Kansas, birds that were specialties of the Mexican border or the coast or Florida or the Far North, and I knew that, to learn about those birds, I would have to go where they lived. So to me it was a simple decision.

To my parents, though, it was anything but simple. All of their friends and relatives were aghast at the idea that a sixteen-year-old would be allowed to leave school and travel halfway across the continent alone. If Dad and Mom had simply bowed to peer pressure, they would have forbidden me to leave. But my parents knew me better than any of their friends or relatives did. I had been the worst troublemaker in the best honors classes, the student council president who got suspended from school for causing trouble, despised by the school administration while getting along well with most of my teachers. I had proven myself responsible and resourceful by living away from home for three summers as the nature counselor at a scout camp while proving myself unwilling to waste any time on things I considered unimportant. My parents had decided that I was never going to follow a normal course of education or career, no matter what happened. And instead of trying to force me into conformity, they were brave enough to let me pursue my own course. I might have been stubborn or determined enough to go even if they had told me not to, but they gave me the most beautiful gift: their permission to travel, their blessings for my independent adventure.

When I first left home at sixteen, I was traveling by Greyhound bus, but I rapidly concluded that bus routes were not designed to take in every birding hot spot and that downtown bus stations were not the best places for birds, or for birders. Before long, I had begun traveling by thumb. This was in the 1970s, and hitchhiking was still commonplace, a standard way of getting around the continent for vast numbers of young people. On any given day in decent weather, every main highway and every major freeway on-ramp would have its own contingent of long-haired young guys with backpacks, standing alone, thumbs raised hopefully, waiting for someone to give them a ride. I became a part of this itinerant throng. With a little patience I could get rides practically anywhere, even remote canyons or isolated wildlife refuges, and I spent the better part of five years crisscrossing North America in pursuit of birds. I hitchhiked to Alaska twice, to Florida and Texas and California dozens of times, always keeping careful notes on the birds and other creatures that I saw. It was a tremendous learning experience. But even though I was focused on learning about birds and nature, along the way I was learning about human nature as well.

And it was fortunate that I was learning, too, because at the beginning of my travels I was extraordinarily naive. In later years I would tell people that hitchhiking was totally safe back then, but of course it wasn't, and the truth is that I came through unscathed because I was just plain lucky. I was in some situations that were genuinely dangerous, times when I feared for my life, and in the wake of such experiences I would be a little more savvy and a little more alert than before.

Of course, I never told my parents about these dangerous situations. Sometimes on my way across the continent I would stop in Wichita, and I would tell Mom and Dad about my adventures, but only the good ones. In my traveler's tales, I was always totally safe, people were always friendly and helpful, the weather was always perfect. I had this idea that I was shielding my parents from the realities of my experience. They believed that I led a charmed life.

Or at the time, at least, I thought that was what they

believed. Not until long afterward did I begin to understand what effect my youthful travels were having on my mother. She never told me herself, either, not even after my thumbing days were over. But my father told me about it years later. "When you were hitchhiking," he said, "your mother would be terrified if the phone rang late at night. Her immediate reaction would be that it must be the state troopers calling, from somewhere, to say that you were in the hospital or in jail, or that you'd been killed. It was always worse for her at night, and she would feel relieved when the sun came up. As if it proved somehow that you had survived overnight. She didn't ever want you to know that. But your mother never had a good night's sleep while you were on the road."

Nightland

There was a time when the realization came to me that my house was not the best place to work on four huge book projects and a dozen magazine stories at once, so I rented a simple office in a building a few miles away. Down the block from this office, there was a large school. In the daytime the school rarely drew my attention; if I went out during the day, I might hear the sounds of the children on the wide open playground, out there every day in the Arizona climate, but they seemed far away. At night, though, if I worked extra-long hours and left the office late, I would hear something else: the voices of killdeers, wild, lonely cries, out there somewhere on that open field in the dark.

I never saw the killdeers there by day. It was a mystery just where these birds came from. There seemed to be no other killdeer habitat for miles around — no undisturbed fields, no muddy shores — and it seemed impossible that those excitable plovers could remain there during the day. Surely the children in their games must run over every square yard of the playground, leaving no place for the killdeers to rest. I had no time to think about it actively, but at the back of my mind, the nighttime presence of those birds was an enduring puzzle. At times under extreme deadline pressure, my schedule would shift and I would arrive at the office at dawn; but if I thought to look out over the schoolyard then, there was no sign of the killdeers. It was as if they had disappeared with first daylight, faded like dreams.

There had been a time, years earlier, when I really had dreamed about killdeers. That was when I was a child myself—an intense little kid bird watcher, stuck in the suburbs, with no binoculars, no transportation, no connection to the bird-watching community except through books. Those books had told me that killdeers were very common birds, but they were not common where I was, not present at all in my little world of a few square blocks. Then one rainy Saturday morning, with no one else about, two had appeared on the field behind my elementary school. I had never seen anything so intense. Even when standing still, the killdeers looked spring-loaded, poised on their toes, poised for flight. I wanted to get closer, but they were watching me with those big dark eyes, and every time I moved they would call in alarm, *dee-dee-deerr*...Finally I must have pressed them too closely, and they were off, in buoyant flight over the rooftops to the west, their cries of *kildeeerrr, kildeeerrrr* floating back to me as they disappeared beyond my young horizon.

I never saw them again on that schoolyard, but I

dreamed about them time after time. In my dreams they were always elusive, running ahead of me, running and pausing to look back, their eyes deep and mysterious. Or they would be flying overhead, trim and elegant on the wing, their wild cries floating down from a great height. I would wake up sometimes thinking for a moment that I had really heard them. And perhaps I had: at that time I did not realize how active, and vocal, the killdeers could be at night. Perhaps they were really flying over, their voices impinging on my sleep, blurring the line between reality and dreams.

We humans, in a natural state, would be creatures of daylight. Our eyes are not adapted for seeing well in dim light, and our other senses are not good enough to compensate. We have had artificial lighting for only a very short time — even our use of fire can't go back more than a few thousand years — and before we had it, our proto-human ancestors would have been ill-equipped to wander about at night. Artificial light has allowed us to invade the dark half of the daily cycle. It has given us the night, in a way, but it has also taken it away, and taken away our sleep.

It was during the time when I was still a kid that I first began to learn about the loss of sleep. I got a paper route to earn money so I could buy more books on natural history, and I would get up at three-thirty every morning to be out there at four, getting all the papers delivered before anyone on the route was awake. Then, of course, I would stay out to see what birds might be stirring at dawn. But as I walked the route in the dark every morning, I began to realize something new about birds: some of them were stirring even before dawn. Although most birds, like humans, are naturally creatures of daylight, a lot of them seemed to be awake at night anyway.

The singing was the most obvious thing. The dawn songs would begin when dawn was just a rumor, before any daylight was visible to my eyes. A robin would start up with a few hesitant phrases in the pitch-black night, then another robin a block away would sing a few phrases more, then others at a distance would join in, and a whole robin chorus would be caroling away by the time the first glimmer of light showed in the east.

Robins were obvious, but western kingbirds, my favorite birds at the time, would start even earlier. They would be repeating their staccato, sputtering dawn song, over and over, an hour before first light. Even earlier than that, some birds would be sounding off. Cardinals sometimes sang a few phrases at any dark hour. The mockingbirds were the most outlandish, of course, often singing all night, especially when the moon was bright. I wondered when they slept, or if they slept at all.

It was the male birds doing the singing, and I had read that they were doing it not merely to provide music but rather to announce and defend their territories. It seemed quixotic, defending against a nonexistent threat: surely, during the hours of darkness, no potential rivals would be invading their territories anyway. So much effort, those mockingbirds singing away in the night, for so little reason. I would think about that on the nights when I stayed awake doing homework, nights when I had a big assignment due the next day. I would stay up focusing on work until it was time to deliver the morning newspapers, then wander into school in a daze, feeling a little high on sleep deprivation, imagining that the mockingbirds must be feeling the same edgy, buzzy sensation.

There was a time a few years later when I realized that the all-night singers like the mockingbirds were hardly the champions of avian sleep deprivation. This was during a period in my late teens and early twenties when I was traveling around North America by bumming rides out on the highways. Standing out on the edge of a busy freeway at night, thumb raised, staring into the oncoming stream of headlights, I would not hear anything but the traffic noise, of course. But if it were a less-traveled road, and if it were spring or fall, I would hear something else. In the quiet times when no vehicles were near, I would hear the call notes of birds floating down from high overhead. They were birds of passage, in swift flight northward in spring or southward in fall, daytime birds migrating at night.

Many of these nocturnal calls merely sounded like generic small birds scattered around the sky, but I recognized the voices of Swainson's thrushes, birds I knew well from seeing them in daylight. Many mornings when I had been out birding in spring or fall, the undergrowth of the woods had seemed full of these shy brown thrushes, stopping over en route between their nesting grounds in the Far North and their wintering grounds deep in the tropics. I knew from my reading that the thrushes were nocturnal migrants, and that many I saw in the mornings would have arrived overnight; but it was different to be out there actually hearing them calling as they passed over, to know that they were traveling at the same time that I was. I was hardly alone. Neither were the thrushes. Warblers, vireos, sparrows, flycatchers, a host of other birds were up there with them, birds of daylight traveling in the dark.

There were many occasions at night when I had been awake too long, when I was tired of waiting for rides, tempted to go off and sleep somewhere. But if the Swainson's thrushes were migrating, I would often just stay awake and keep trying, thinking that if they could do it, so could I. The thrushes were no more creatures of the night than I was, but they were awake, traveling hard under their own power. In the morning we would all be tired and a little strange from the tingly rush of lost sleep, and it would give me the illusion of having a common bond with the migrant birds.

There was a time when I was finishing work on my first book, and I stayed awake for something like five days straight. I had been working on that book for more than six years, but at the end it came down to a few weeks of intense concentration and then a final marathon of insane focus. The book was called *A Field Guide to Advanced Birding*, and although the early research had indeed involved a lot of birding, the latter stages involved just words and pictures, ink on paper. I had no margin for being late: at a specific hour on a certain date, I was getting on a plane and crossing the Pacific, to be gone leading tours for months, and if the book were not finished before I left for that trip, it seemed unlikely the publisher would ever accept it. I simply had to finish the book. I felt like a small bird migrating over hostile terrain at night, with no choice but to keep going.

During that time, I was too mentally wired up to sleep: if I lay down, my mind would be racing a mile a minute with details and ideas, and I would soon get up again. So instead of trying to take short naps, I took short walks, out around the streets and hills of the neighborhood. While I walked, I would be thinking about the birds in the book I was finishing: warblers, sparrows, hawks, sandpipers, loons, flycatchers, and all the rest. It was September, and if I were walking at night, I could imagine some of those same birds migrating overhead. I thought of all of us as traveling together, awake in the night when we should have been asleep, living on adrenaline, pushing on toward an unseen destination.

In *One Hundred Years of Solitude,* the amazing novel by Nobel laureate Gabriel García Márquez, there is an episode in which the villagers of Macondo all develop insomnia. Total insomnia: they are simply awake all the time, going about their business day and night. They're not particularly bothered by this condition, except for one problem. With the lack of sleep, they are all steadily losing their memories as well.

Of course, García Márquez has earned the literary license to draw whatever connections he pleases, but I don't think memory is the thing that goes when we don't sleep. I think what we lose is a kind of mental innocence. Although I hate to say it, maybe we lose our youth that way, not through the physical drain of failing to rest but through the knowledge that comes with having our eyes open too long, seeing too much. The expression about "sleeping like a baby" may ring true: perhaps if we never lost sleep we would never get any older. But it's too late for me to find that out.

Even as I am writing these words, I am stealing time from another project that should be more pressing: I'm deep into the deadline pressure of finishing another book. I have been awake most of the time for the last three weeks. It has become just like the final stages of all my other books. It's my own fault that I'm in this situation, a result of poor planning, taking on too many projects at once. Looking back, though, I have to wonder when this started, when I got the idea that I could accomplish more by sleeping less. I have to wonder when I developed this passion to write about nature, to share it with others, to the extent that it sometimes precludes my going out and experiencing nature myself. I have to wonder how pursuing a dream could take away the possibility of sleeping and dreaming any further.

Regardless, at this point there's no turning back. Like a night migrant, I must keep going. I have to get the current book done by the deadline or it will cause problems for everyone, the publisher and the printers and the binders and the marketing people and the distributors and the bookstores, all the way down the line, and I dare not let that happen. As I leave my office at three in the morning, I can hear, from down the street, the voices of the killdeers, wild and lonely, somewhere out on that schoolyard in the dark. Or are they really there at all? Maybe I am only hearing echoes of my own lost childhood, crying out in the wilderness of the night.

KOKAKO
SUNRISE

WHAT IS the most beautiful birdsong in the world?

That's not a fair question, and it would not be fair to answer — at least, not without hearing every song first. All of these birdsongs should be heard in live performances, too, in the wild, not in zoos or on recordings, because a bird's voice cannot be fully appreciated until it is heard in its natural setting. But no one person will ever see every one of the world's ten thousand species of birds, let alone hear their songs. Too many of those birds are rare, localized, elusive creatures; one human life is not time enough to track down every single one.

Of course, it would be a beautiful challenge to *try* to hear all of them. And one would get to hear some wonderful bird voices in the process. Some of the finalists in this contest would be right here in North America. For example, someone who favored simplicity might lean toward the song of the varied thrush: long, single whistles with a haunting, breathy quality, lingering in the green shadows of northwestern forests. A person who liked complexity might think of the winter wren, with its rushing cascade of sweet trilled notes. Others might prefer the fox sparrow, or the hermit thrush, or the sky lark, or some other vocalist. But picking a personal favorite is not the same as nominating the most beautiful birdsong in the world.

So my question is one that no person can fairly answer. Having admitted that, though, I have an answer for it anyway. I have listened to birds on seven continents and dozens of islands, and I believe the world's most beautiful birdsong is that of the kokako, a forest dweller of New Zealand. That answer is touched with sadness, however, because the kokako is scarce and becoming scarcer, its unearthly song heard less often with every passing year.

The people who settled New Zealand never tried to mistreat their wildlife — at least, no more than other pioneers did in any other part of the world.

The Maoris, the graceful warriors who were the first to arrive, may have hunted the great flightless moas into extinction. But in general they observed and appreciated nature, and their names for many of the native trees and birds are still used today. Later, when white settlement came, most of the pioneers were of British descent, and they brought with them a fondness for nature. There was nothing intentional about the catastrophe they caused.

The problem was that this land in its natural state had been simply too benign. In its long, long isolation, New

Zealand had developed a fauna that was almost totally free from predators. There were no snakes, no land mammals. Flightless birds flourished, with no need to take to the air for safety. Other birds that fed in the treetops would descend to the ground to nest and raise their young. The original ecosystem here was as gentle as the Garden of Eden, and as easily overturned.

The first wave of extinction came with small predators brought by the white settlers. Weasels, cats, and the ever-present rats came in on the coattails of Europeans and began systematically to wipe out the native bird life. The unsuspicious New Zealand thrush, feeding on the ground, was unprepared for the likes of rats. The tiny Stephens Island wren was discovered, and exterminated, by the lighthouse keeper's cat. The big flightless parrot was a pitifully easy target when it was nesting. The side effects of civilization that would have spelled a minor problem elsewhere turned into a disaster for many of the birds of New Zealand.

Many of the most vulnerable birds succumbed quickly. But in the wake of this initial destruction, New Zealand developed some of the world's most ardent conservationists, skilled in the management and rescue of endangered species. On small offshore islands free from predators, they have established populations of birds that otherwise would be extinct. Several species have been lost forever, but others, like the saddleback and the stitchbird, are thriving in these island sanctuaries.

On the big islands that are referred to as the "mainland" of New Zealand, many birds that do not nest on the ground have managed to survive the wave of introduced predators. There seems to be no immediate cause for concern over the whitehead, the gray warbler, the New Zealand brown creeper, or various other endemics; they are surviving in the patches of native vegetation, and even spreading into exotic plantings. But something of a mystery surrounds the kokako. Even in stands of forest that have never been cut, the kokako seems to be in a long, slow decline.

What is the kokako? Well, for starters, it is not like any bird you've ever seen. One of only two surviving members of the New Zealand wattlebird family, it is shaped something like a small crow or a large, short-tailed jay. Its plumage is entirely soft gray, and its only notable mark is a small blue wattle at the corner of the bill. (The kokako is only half the bird it used to be: the form on the South Island, which had orange wattles instead of blue, is now apparently extinct.) Indeed, it is sometimes called "blue-wattled crow." But the comparison to a crow is shaky at best—unless you can imagine a crow that goes bounding about among the branches in dense rainforest, stopping to sing the most unbelievable music.

Although I've been back to see it again since, I still have vivid memories of my first encounter with the kokako.

That was years ago, during a birding tour that I was helping to lead. I had been only mildly interested in going to New Zealand in the first place, but as the trip progressed, I was rapidly falling in love with that island nation and its bird life.

In theory, finding a kokako should be easy, if you know where to look: the birds are incredibly faithful to specific sites. Off the record, some researchers told us that they thought a kokako might live twenty years or more, and might spend its entire adult life in one spot.

Our first attempt for the species was in far northern New Zealand, when we went to the forest remnant of Puketi with a local biologist. This man knew the location of one bird, had known it for some time, and could predict exactly where it would be. A pair had lived at this spot, but the female of the pair had disappeared. For six years now the male had remained, singing in vain, waiting for the mate that never came. In a sad irony, this male had developed an attraction to humans. Researchers had gone to the area and played tape recordings, hoping to elicit a response from the bird, and the kokako, hearing the voice of its own kind, had come in eagerly to look. Now if the researchers visited the area, they no longer played tapes. But this bird still made the association between people and its own species, and it would come and follow the biologists around, as if in a desperate search for company. But we could not get to the spot where this individual lived—recent rains had made the road impassable for many miles—and we came away with nothing but a heightened sense of mystery about this bird.

More determined than before, we contacted Brent Calder, another biologist who had studied the kokako. He recommended a spot and agreed to join us. So a few days later we drove out, well before daylight, to the forest patch of Pureora.

New Zealand has produced a remarkable breed of field researchers who work under rugged conditions, with little funding but with vast amounts of determination, studying rare birds to find the path to their survival. Calder was one of these tough fieldmen. He saw the native birds as an integral part of the native forest, and he clearly loved this forest. As we stood shivering in the predawn chill, he pointed out the silhouettes of the local trees with their strange-sounding Maori names: rimu, totara, matai, miro, kahikatea. Worthy surroundings for a kokako. Under the trees stretched a maze of shrubs, a tangle of vines, a riot of ferns, all dense and lush and green. No wonder—according to Calder, it rained on two days out of three at Pureora Forest. We were lucky today; the sky was clear.

And as the first rays of the rising sun touched the treetops, we heard the sound. At first it was almost unbelievable: this rich, sweet chord floating through the trees could not have come from the throat of a bird; no, it was church music, an organ playing in the cathedral of the forest. Then the sound came again, a different chord, followed by two soft, deliberate notes. Then another chord. It was stunning. I had known that a songbird's vocal structure, the syrinx, is capable of making two different sounds at once, but never had I heard this ability used so obviously or to such musical effect.

Calder led us quietly into the forest. It was slow going. We had to thread our way through the trees and around the worst of the tangles: this forest remnant was strictly protected, and no new trails were to be cut. A hundred yards into the deep green interior of the forest, we paused in a slight opening among the trees.

From far away we could hear another kokako tuning up. The bird closer at hand seemed unaffected, continuing with its unhurried music. The notes were rich and pure, the pauses between them sometimes long and deliberate, with a sense of being carefully controlled. It made me think of some keyboard virtuoso, in a peaceful and contemplative mood, sitting at a church organ and slowly improvising. Every so often, as if to remind us that it was, in fact, a bird, the kokako would toss in an odd clucking or mewing note, but these stray sounds hardly spoiled the effect.

All around New Zealand I had been carrying a tape recorder, recording the songs of many birds for my own reference, but seldom playing them back in the field. Surrounded by endangered species as we were, it seemed unwise to do anything that might disturb the birds. Now I was recording the kokako. I had not intended to play back the tape out loud, but Calder motioned that I should: "Just a little of it, softly," he said. "That will do the trick."

When I complied, it seemed at first that the tape had had no effect. Then the tone of the bird's song began to change. Instead of the long, organ-toned phrases, the kokako was giving shorter, low-pitched notes, with an inquiring or conversational sound. Now Calder was whistling back to it. The kokako seemed to be moving toward us, and then abruptly it stopped singing altogether.

When shy forest birds come in to imitations, they are often very quiet on their final approach, so the silence made us fully alert. And something moved. Not far away, at the limit of what we could see through the latticework of vegetation, something was moving through the upper branches. But it could not be a bird—at least, not any bird we knew. It was bounding along limbs, leaping from one branch to another, agile as a monkey, silent as a shadow, tracing a great circle around the point where we stood. Then this thing launched into the air from a tree-top, on wings that made a sharp rustling sound, loud and abrupt in the stillness. It was the kokako.

Brent Calder whistled to the bird again. He knew its moods, knew which notes would bring a response of curiosity, not challenge. So the kokako came back, bounding and hopping and creeping through the branches, peering at us with one big eye and then the other. It was a larger bird than I had expected, trim but sturdy, with strong legs and a stout black bill. The blue wattles at the corners of its mouth gave it a bizarre expression. By instinct we all stood still, hardly breathing, as this strange bird came close. Then it was off again, with a loud, rapid-fire rustling of wings, and a minute later it began to sing again in the distance.

Quietly we picked our way back out of the forest and onto the road. By now the sun was well above the horizon, but it seemed this kokako might sing all day. The song was richer than ever, with deep, full tones and harmonious phrases, and now the bird was working its way up through a tall totara tree that rose above the forest canopy. From the road we were able to spot its highest song perch, and we trained a telescope on it as it sang, almost surrounded by foliage, continuing its concert of improvised organ music.

As we listened, we wondered what the future held for this enigmatic singer. Even where the forest remains uncut, even where it nests well above the dangers on the ground, the kokako may face a threat from — of all things — deer and possums. Brushtail possums from Australia, and deer of several nationalities, have been set loose on the land in New Zealand. These seemingly "harmless" vegetarians are changing the forests forever. And since the kokako also feeds heavily on plant material, it is coming into direct competition with these hardy invaders. It seems there is no end to the damage that can be done by the alien animals, no end to the challenges facing the conservationists who work to save what is left of their original paradise.

I still have the tape recording that I made of the kokako at sunrise in Pureora Forest. Any time I listen to it now, I have to repeat the assertion I made earlier: this is the most beautiful birdsong on our planet. If it were gone, I can't begin to imagine what species I would nominate to take its place. I'll just have to trust that the New Zealanders will succeed in keeping this bird alive, so I won't have to face that decision.

"DOESN'T IT SEEM like a miracle," my mother asked, "that your birds should have such beautiful songs? So much more beautiful than they would have to be.... It's like a special blessing."

I couldn't disagree, so I just nodded.

"My dad...your grandfather Bader...used to whistle at the chickadees. I've told you that. When we lived in Iowa. And they would sing back to him." She made her own weak attempt to whistle and then thought better of it. I waited a moment and then whistled an imitation of the black-capped chickadee's song, *seee-bee-eee*. Mom's eyes misted up a little.

"They do whistle back at you," I said. "Chickadees are great that way. They'll countersing with you. If you do it with the second note a little off-key, they'll whistle back with the right pitch, time after time. Almost as if they were trying to correct your performance."

"I thought I heard them...a few times...at the house here." She looked at me as if she were waiting to be contradicted. "I know...you've told me, they weren't in that neighborhood. But it didn't hurt to listen for them. Just in case."

"Sure," I said weakly. "Birds have wings."

"Even penguins," she said, giggling.

"Yeah, yeah. Even penguins. Even ostriches. Even flightless steamer ducks. Leftovers from the evolutionary process." I was thinking about our attempts to get her to move from this sterile downtown rehab center to the care facility run by the Presbyterians. That place was in a shady old neighborhood with big trees, and probably there were chickadees in those trees. It might even have been possible to put up a bird feeder outside her window there. If only we had been able to persuade her to move.

When Mom had come out of her coma, she had been in the hospital for weeks, and then the doctors had moved her to this rehab center just a couple of blocks away. She had cried about leaving the hospital. Apparently in her short time there she had already grown attached to the nurses and other staff on that wing. And eventually it dawned on us that the same thing was happening on the fourth floor of the rehab center.

As the weeks started to turn into months at the center, as we started to wonder about the actual amount of rehabilitation and therapy being applied there, my brothers began looking around Wichita for other places where Mom might get better care. Advice from the minister at my parents' old church led them to a place that seemed ideal. We conferred about it and agreed: the surroundings there would be far more pleasant, and it would be well worth the extra money.

But when JB went to tell her about it, he ran into a snag: she didn't want to go. At that point Mom was still struggling to make herself understood, but she was as adamant as her strength would allow her to be, and the message was that she didn't want to move from where she was.

In some consternation, we all discussed what to do next. Rick's wife, Carla, insisted that we should not even hint at making Mom do anything against her will, and we all agreed; she was already in a situation of feeling powerless, and we could not take away the last few things over which she had any control. Ralph suggested trying to take her over to the other place for a visit, but the logistics of moving Mom anywhere were formidable, and besides, she said she didn't even want to visit. JB tried describing the other place in glowing terms and showing her photos and brochures, but she wasn't interested. Rick finally nailed it. "She doesn't want anything to change. Think about what's happened to her the last couple of years. Dad dying. Her having more health problems. Her stroke. Going from the hospital to this dump. Every change she's gone through has been a change for the worse. No matter what we say, she doesn't want anything more to change."

So, uneasily, we left the situation as it was. Periodically we would mention the possibility of moving, just in case she had changed her mind, but Mom never wavered on this question.

We all respected her too much to argue with her. She had always had a quality of poise and dignity. This had been noticeable but not too surprising when she was still young and strong, but it was startling to see how she maintained this air of dignified grace even when she was physically wasted and weak. The nurses and other staff people might bustle about obliviously, acting as if many of the rehab center residents were vegetables or troublesome pets, but eventually they would catch on to my mother's steely resolve to be herself and they would begin to treat her with more respect. Physically she was a wreck. Spiritually she was a lady of elegance and strong will.

It had been a saying when she was young that no one had ever won an argument with a member of her family, and if they had, they never would have known it. My father's side of the family was equally strong-willed, and my brothers and I apparently all inherited the same tendency. ("I'm not stubborn," I used to tell my parents. "You can call me stubborn every day for a hundred years and I'll never admit to it.") So within our family, we usually chose not to argue at all, knowing it would be pointless. In earlier discussions about the Galápagos Islands, I had tried to explain to my mother the basics of adaptive radiation and evolution by natural selection, to no avail. She understood everything I was saying, she could grasp the concepts perfectly well, she just chose not to believe that this was how things had happened. I realized much later that it wouldn't have mattered if I had broken the news to her about Galápagos penguins being unable to fly. She might not have argued openly with her bird-expert son, she might have nodded her head, but she would have gone on believing what she wanted to believe.

It occurred to me that when my hero, Roger Tory Peterson, had been in the Galápagos, he had produced a documentary film about the islands, and he had called it *Galápagos: Wild Eden*. I had not thought anything of the title when I first heard it, assuming that the reference to Eden was simply a convenient shorthand term for a wild and unspoiled place, but later it dawned on me that this specific title must have been chosen with more care than that. There had to have been something deliberate in going to these islands, to ground zero for evolutionary theory, and making a direct reference to the Garden of Eden as described in the book of Genesis and the story of the creation. Of course Roger understood the facts of evolution and was not denying them, but he seemed to hint that in his worldview there was still room for miracles.

And I, so sure of myself and of the unshakable veracity of the things I had read just yesterday, still had to come up against the limits of my own knowledge. So determined to be accurate and scientific, I could not prove scientifically that miracles did not exist.

ABUNDANT
LIFE

FOR SEVERAL YEARS, Victor Emanuel and I taught a workshop on bird migration every spring on the upper Texas coast, east of Houston, where the coastline runs straight east toward the Louisiana border. For northbound birds coming across the Gulf of Mexico, this would be the first land they would see, some twelve to eighteen hours after they had departed the Yucatán Peninsula. If the weather were good, most of those migrants would not stop at the immediate coast. They would fly many miles inland, so that even on days when millions of birds were flying, their numbers would be swallowed up in the hundreds of square miles of woodlands in the interior. Only when the weather was bad would the struggling migrants stop as soon as they hit the coast. Then we would witness a classic "fallout," with orioles and tanagers festooning every bush, warblers swarming in every tree, an awesome demonstration of the sheer numbers that would ordinarily pass overhead.

The nearest hotels large enough to hold our workshop groups were up along Interstate 10, so every morning we would load our vans for the short drive south to the coast. And every morning, driving down Highway 124, I would notice a building positioned alongside the road, its sign out front where I couldn't miss it: Abundant Life Church.

I never stopped to talk to the pastor or the congregation, so I never had the chance to tell them how they had affected my perceptions. Over time, the beautiful name of their church had become linked, in my sleepy early-morning mind, with the spectacle of migration that we were studying. I hoped they would realize that I meant no disrespect. After all, there are many ways in which a life can be blessed with abundance. For any naturalist, for anyone alive in the outdoors, abundant life — an abundance of living things — is worth celebrating.

It's a basic truth about those of us who are bird watchers: we like variety. We like rarity. We like to go out and see a lot of different kinds of birds, and if some of them are rare, meaning we see very few of them, so much the better. Appreciating sheer numbers of things may be a little more difficult.

Maybe it's inevitable that we would place value on rarity. But it is unfortunate that the counterpoint to this tendency is expressed as lack of respect for anything common. I've fallen prey to this myself. I wince when I recall hearing myself say, "Oh, it's only a cardinal," as if there were something bad about a gorgeous flaming red bird that will perch up high and sing out rich whistles even against a bleak landscape of winter. If the cardinal were a rare bird, we would climb mountains to see it, and we would gasp with excitement when we finally got a good look. Why should we dismiss it as uninteresting just because it's always outside the kitchen window? We should value it all the more because it enhances our lives every day. But it's so easy to take birds for granted when they're easy to see.

If we dismiss the common birds, even worse is our tendency to have actual contempt for those that are more than merely common. So many times I have heard people say that they hate birds like grackles, perhaps, or starlings, or even house finches or Canada geese. When I ask how they can use a term like "hate," they have trouble articulating the reasons, but generally it comes down to the fact that these birds are so numerous. So what's wrong with that? Grackles are native birds here, and I still recall how they thrilled me when I was six years old: seeing common grackles up close and admiring their vivid, iridescent colors and staring pale eyes, or seeing their huge flocks streaming over in late summer, rivers of grackles in purposeful flight toward nighttime roosts. But some people dislike them simply because they do occur in huge flocks. Likewise with starlings: we may fall back on the argument that they are not native here, or that they compete with other birds for nest sites, but for many people the dislike is rooted in sheer numbers. Canada geese are magnificent birds, and house finches are beautiful little songsters, and both were popular at one time until their populations increased beyond a certain point. Then they became objects of scorn for many people.

An appreciation for abundant creatures may be an acquired taste. Yes, if you see a literal million flamingos ringing a shallow lake, as I have a couple of times in Africa, that blizzard of pink is bound to take your breath away. But big numbers of less spectacular creatures may not seem impressive at first. It may require some study, some careful philosophical thought, for us to come to the point where we can fully appreciate those living things that are truly abundant. Sometimes, even as confirmed bird watchers, we need to step out onto a different plane and consider other kinds of living things.

I saw abundance on a higher level and in a different light one summer evening on an island in Lake Erie. I was seriously in love, and I was actively courting a young woman named Kim, who was the education director for a bird observatory in northwestern Ohio. The observatory was holding its annual Nature Day Camp for teenagers, and I volunteered to go along for the one overnight camp-out of the session. I had talked to the kids about birds earlier, but on this night I was supposed to talk about moths, putting up a black light to attract a few of the colorful species of moth life in the area. As it turned out, the black light was superfluous, and we had a chance to experience insect life in a way that was sublime and magnificent just because of where we were.

Our camp-out was in a state park on South Bass Island. We had gone there because it was a good campground on an attractive island. Lake Erie is not the largest of the Great Lakes, but it does cover nearly ten thousand square miles, enough to be its own major ecosystem. The lake was seriously polluted in decades past, but dogged efforts by environmentalists have succeeded in cleaning up the waters to a remarkable degree. That improvement in water quality is a fact, not just local hype. We have independent evidence, because the local mayfly populations have rebounded to something like their former abundance.

Burrowing mayflies of the genus *Hexagenia* spend about 99.7 percent of their lives underwater, digging around in fine silt on the lake floor. When they finally emerge and fly away, their remaining time is so brief that the entire mayfly order is called Ephemeroptera — ephemeral wings. After a year or two of burrowing around in the comfortable ooze below the water, these small creatures are driven by instinct to clamber up into the alien element of the air, there to dance in flight and make love and then die, leaving behind them the eggs of the next generation. Because their time is so brief, they must somehow be coordinated in mass emergences, with many taking to the sky at once. Those who miss the dance will miss their best chance to mate, and their genes will not be passed on.

I knew all that, but somehow it had not clicked in my mind when I got on the ferry to head out to South Bass Island to join Kim and the other camp counselors and the kids. I had not looked out at the square miles of water that the ferry was crossing, the square miles of water around the island, and thought about them as mayfly nurseries. But as dusk began to settle over the campground, something began to dawn as well: the realization that we might be there for the mass emergence.

Only a few hundred of them were around the campground at first, not enough to make a major impression. The kids had all seen mayflies before, because, out of the hundreds of species, there are a few around on almost any warm day. And single mayflies are soft-bodied, slow-flying little things, about as harmless and innocuous as insects can be. They can't sting. They can't bite. They can't defend themselves at all, except by fluttering away weakly on filmy wings. For the *Hexagenia* species, at least, the best defense is in sheer abundance, blanketing the area with such vast numbers that predators cannot make a dent in the population.

I had read about events of decades past, in lakefront cities such as Green Bay and Chicago and Toledo, when city crews had been dispatched with heavy equipment to clear away mounds of dead mayflies four or five feet deep. And these were only the mayflies that had died over land, not over the water where they would have gone to lay their eggs. But these utterly harmless insects, because of their sheer numbers, had been branded a "nuisance" in several cities. Some people even were relieved when the mayfly populations crashed, instead of interpreting this correctly as a sign that their local waters were dangerously polluted. When the *Hexagenia* mayflies built back up to abundance in western Lake Erie, any thinking person should have rejoiced that the lake was becoming healthier again.

We tried talking to the kids a little about that idea, and then Kim and the other counselors went back to keeping them occupied with storytelling and journal entries and other camp things. I mostly watched the mayflies, and periodically the kids would join me, staring up at the spectacle overhead. That night the clouds of mayflies over the lake would show up on weather radar in Toledo and Detroit, but it was more impressive to be right there, to see this in real life. Around and above the campsite, just above treetop level, more and more and more mayflies joined the swarms, fluttering up and down in magical silence. Looking up through the swarms with binoculars and gradually focusing farther away, we could see layer upon layer of them, a dancing throng extending into the sky. There were thousands above each tree, hundreds of thousands visible at once from where we stood, possibly billions over the island as a whole.

By this time tomorrow night, the female mayflies would have dispersed out over the lake to lay their eggs, trillions of eggs. Only a small percentage of those eggs would result in adults taking part in next year's dance. Most of the hatchling mayflies would wind up as food for fish or tadpoles or dragonfly nymphs or any number of other aquatic creatures. For all their abundance, they formed only one strand in a grand web of interactions in the natural world.

Watching them on this night, we were thinking less about the science of this ecological web than about the magic of the spectacle. These silent millions dancing in the sky had no time to lose. They were ephemeral creatures caught up in eternal mysteries, making the most of their brief moment in the sky, choosing a mate out of that swirling mass in what seemed like an act of faith in the future. All the kids and Kim and I stood together, as silent and reverent as if we were in church, gazing upward and trying to comprehend this abundance of life.

THE BEACH
IS BAD

EVERY BARRIER BEACH is a changeable work of art, a sand sculpture created by winds and tides. Every barrier beach is a work in progress. All along our sandy Atlantic Coast are peninsulas that were once islands, islands that were once shoals, inlets that were once solid beaches. Some lighthouses on the sand have toppled into the sea, others stand marooned a mile inland as currents and winds continue to reshape the topography of the coastline. Humans are drawn to barrier beaches as to beaches everywhere, and we may even build roads and towns there, but they last only until the sea decides to take them away.

On this continent, the granddaddy of all barrier beaches is the great arc of the Outer Banks of North Carolina. At their northern end, near the Virginia border, the banks are separated from the marshy mainland coast by only a few miles of open water. South of Kitty Hawk and Manteo, though, the banks arch out to the southeast and then south, a narrow strip of sand running straight south for miles, while the mainland coast falls away toward the southwest. At the end of their long southward stretch, where the banks angle sharply west again at Cape Hatteras, the mainland lies thirty miles away across Pamlico Sound. When you stand at Cape Hatteras, you are really thirty miles offshore, on a temporary and insignificant bit of sand dominated by the sea.

Given their fortunate position, the Outer Banks are a favorite point of departure for birding boat trips on the ocean. One-day trips offshore there can easily reach the Gulf Stream, and North Carolina has become famous as the best place on our Atlantic Coast for viewing rare seabirds. I have gone offshore there on a number of occasions. My most recent attempt was during an October trip, when I went to speak at a conference in Virginia Beach, down at the southeastern corner of the state of Virginia and just across the state line from the northern end of the Outer Banks. I was now engaged to Kim, that wonderful girl from Ohio, and she had never been on a serious seabird trip, so she came with me. The conference would end on Friday, and my friend Brian Patteson was running an organized birding boat trip off Hatteras on Saturday, so the timing seemed ideal.

Violent storms moved into the coastal area during the week, and from our conference center in Virginia Beach we watched the weather, hoping the storms would clear out before the weekend. Day after day they lingered. Not until Friday afternoon did it appear that the weather would break. Doggedly optimistic, we drove south toward Hatteras.

By late that evening, on the Outer Banks themselves, we could see that conditions were still bad. The rain had ceased, but wind was still whipping from the northwest, and the ocean was a roiling mass of waves and spray. I remembered having read that the dunes east of the road were mostly artificial, piled up in an attempt to keep the sea from washing over two-lane Highway 12. If so, the dunes were failing in their assignment. There was water across the road in several places, and near the town of Rodanthe, as it was getting dark, the highway was underwater for at least half a mile, deep enough that I wondered if our little rental car would make it.

Sometime during the evening I called Brian Patteson, and was not surprised to learn that the seabird trip had been postponed at least until Sunday. The boat captains on the Outer Banks are tough, but they're not dumb, and they know when it's too rough to take a group out. But Brian said we had probably driven the worst sections of the highway already, so Kim and I continued slowly south to Hatteras, picking our way through more flooded spots in the dark.

After our arrival late in the stormy night, it was a shock to wake up Saturday to brilliant sunshine. There was still a north wind at dawn, but it diminished to a breeze by midday. We looked for birds in some patches of woods near town and then headed to the outermost point of Cape Hatteras.

The shape of the cape changes with every season, but the basic outline is dominated by the outer beach running straight south to Cape Hatteras Point, the shoreline angling from there back toward the northwest. Within the angle of the point is a large salt pond that always has lots of gulls and shorebirds, and we decided to go there to see if any odd strays had come in on the storm. The paved road ended well short of the end of the point, and from there the fishermen would drive their trucks down the outer beach. One look was enough to convince us not to try the beach in our rental car. We parked at the end of the pavement and walked.

The sea has a longer memory than the sky. Overhead the sky was calm and blue, but the sea was still an angry gray, churning violently and sending huge waves smashing onto the beach. We soon saw other reminders of the stormy weather. As we walked a trail south through the dunes, we began flushing small birds out of the dry beach grass. Palm warblers were out there, and myrtle warblers, and then a junco, so tired that it barely hopped out of our way. Then a flicker came up out of the grass, a chunky brown woodpecker looking disoriented as it flew around with not a tree in sight. These were all migrant birds, we guessed, blown off course by the weather of the preceding week.

While we were watching the flicker, it suddenly made a panicked dive into the grass just as a shadow swept in front of us, and we looked up to see a peregrine falcon cruising overhead in fast, level flight. This big, angular-winged falcon was a bird I had half expected. Most other birds of prey do not migrate in any numbers down the southeastern coastal plain. There are a lot of hawks at coastal points south to Cape May, New Jersey, and even as far south as Cape Charles, Virginia, but south of there they mostly cut inland. Chunky, soaring buteos like red-tailed hawk and fluttering forest birds like sharp-shinned hawk will avoid going over water if they can, so they stay away from places like the Outer Banks. But the powerful peregrine crosses open water without hesitation, and it is a regular sight all along the barrier beaches in migration.

We watched the falcon disappear over the dunes ahead of us. A minute later, Kim said, "It's coming back." I picked it up immediately, zooming along low to our right, barely above eye level, quickly vanishing behind us. I started to say, "That was a great look," when Kim said, "Oh, there are two of them!" And I realized that she was looking in a completely different direction, watching two peregrines high to our left.

From then on we had peregrines in view almost con-tinuously — usually one or two, sometimes four or five or even six visible at once — probably the same half dozen birds patrolling the area of the point. And what a show they put on, sometimes whipping past in low-level flight, sometimes circling high with wings and tail fully spread, sometimes chasing and dodging with one another, some-times power-diving from on high. It was the ultimate avian air show. For the rest of the afternoon, whatever else we were seeing, we kept looking up to admire the pere-grines.

At the salt pond near the end of the point, as expected, we found gulls and terns resting. Hundreds of gulls were there, and dozens of terns, all standing with their bills pointed into the breeze. On this day they were almost all of the larger varieties: great black-backed and lesser black-backed and herring gulls, Caspian and royal and Sandwich terns. The smaller types of terns were entirely absent, and the smaller gulls were nearly so; we wondered if they might have moved out ahead of the rough weather. Their larger relatives had no reason to fear the storms. Masters of the wind, they would have been here anyway, far out over the continental shelf, even if the Outer Banks had not existed. Groups of birds were coming and going even as we watched, loose parties of gulls, little squadrons of terns, sweeping in to land or taking off and heading out over the horizon.

After studying the birds on the salt pond, we walked over to the outer beach, lined with fishermen's trucks, the anglers themselves now mostly occupied with drinking beer rather than trying to fish in that roiling surf. We were trying to scan the ocean for seabirds, but the high waves and flying spray made it hard to see any distance; the wind-driven wave tops seemed to reach far higher than our eye level. Somehow, Kim spotted a tiny bird flying in our direction. When she got me onto it, the bird was still at least fifty yards offshore, flying straight toward us from out over the ocean. It came closer and closer, barely clearing the tops of the waves, then veered off to our left, and finally plopped down on the open beach.

It was a palm warbler, and it was clearly exhausted. We could surmise what had happened: this tiny migrant had been blown offshore sometime, perhaps last night, and it had just now found its way back to land. It might have been out over the water for twelve or eighteen hours or even longer, beating its tiny wings untold thousands of times, forced to keep flying or die, until it finally arrived at the salvation of dry land.

During the afternoon we saw other migrants sitting exhausted on the beach, or actually saw them come in from over the water: more palm warblers, myrtle warblers, a lone white-crowned sparrow. We watched one common yellowthroat arrive from over the ocean and fly right past us. Weak with exhaustion, struggling along just a few inches above the sand, it appeared to be aiming for the shelter of the beach grass at the dune line. Unfortunately, it chose a route right through the center of the resting gull flock at the salt pond. Kim and I both reacted like the audience at a scary film when the characters on the screen are about to make a predictably bad move: *"No! Don't go in there!"* Any one of the gulls could have swallowed the yellowthroat with one gulp. Miraculously, they all ignored this easy morsel, and the tired bird made it to the safety of the dunes.

The smallest migrant we saw on the beach was a golden-crowned kinglet, a microbird barely more than three inches long. Seeking shelter under the lawn chairs of a family lounging by their truck, it attracted the attention of two young children. We were too far away to hear the conversation, but the body language was obvious. Kids: "Daddy! Look!" Dad, bored and dismissive: "Aaahh, it's just a bird." *There's real ignorance for you,* I thought. *Your kids are smarter than you are, pal; at least they're paying attention to the real world.*

Kim and I talked for a while about the little songbird migrants we were seeing, tried to imagine what they had gone through: perhaps taking off from somewhere in Maryland or Pennsylvania at dusk the day before, north of the storm track, heading south under deceptively calm conditions overnight, then getting caught up in the weather and wind-drifted offshore. Being out over the ocean at dawn, nothing visible but sky and frenzied waves, terrifying surroundings for such small birds. Reorienting by their internal compasses and beating back to the west, back toward land, hours and hours across the open water. If the Outer Banks had not been here, it seemed doubtful they could have made it another thirty miles to the mainland. For a bird as tiny as this golden-crowned kinglet, it would have been a challenge of monstrous proportions. It seemed to us that even the most obtuse beer drinkers on the beach should have been able to muster some respect for this intrepid little survivor, if only they had known, for the possibility that it might have just gone through a harrowing test of endurance beyond human imagination.

Another fisherman, though, gave us our quote of the day. Kim and I had tried to go back to our car by following the outer beach, but the growing waves had forced us to detour up through the soft sand of the steep-sided dunes. We were wondering about all those Jeeps and monster pickups at the point, wondering how they were going to get back out again, when we came across a man who had just done it. The wet sand splattered all over his truck suggested that it had not been easy. Another guy just arriving in a truck, considering whether to drive out that narrow strip of wave-pounded beach, stopped to consult with the first man. It seemed that the obvious answer would have been "Well, duhh!" But the burly, sunburned fisherman put it in more colorful terms. "The beach is *bad*," he bellowed, in a rich baritone, drawling it out so that "bad" was at least a two-syllable word. We were so taken by the sound that we adopted it as a catch phrase for all manner of situations. Ultimately, after Kim and I were married, the phrase went all around the family, and months later our niece Hannah was still greeting us with "The beach is bad!"

We didn't mean it, though. It was a matter of perspective, and we had been given the chance to see this barrier beach from the perspective of other lives besides our own. This could be a casual interruption in a familiar ocean world, a last hope of rescue in a terrifying wilderness, an aerial playground, a place of refuge, a place of wonder.

THE WINDOW in that room faced the east. Often in the morning the staff would close the drapes to shut out the glare of the Kansas sun, but much of the time the drapes were fully open, letting in a view to break the unrelenting whiteness of the room. From her position, lying down in bed on the fourth floor, my mother was not able to see very much except sky outside that window. But she watched that sky all the same.

When I was visiting, I would usually stay late into the evening before going off to one of my brothers' houses or to a motel to sleep. Often the drapes would be partly open at night—there was no one outside the fourth floor to see in anyway—and I imagined that my mother would be watching that window at the approach of dawn, after another fitful and uncomfortable night, watching for the first hint of sunrise, waiting to see the sunrise colors and waiting for the rehab center to start to stir.

My father had been gone more than two years, and she ached with missing him, she missed him all the time, but she told me once that she thought of him especially in the sunrise. She prayed a lot these days. She hinted that she was wondering how many sunrises and sunsets she would have to endure before God took her away to be with her husband again. But then she would be overcome with the sense that it was sinful to be thinking that way, and she would focus on her sons again, listening to our voices and searching our faces for reflections of our father, of the man she had married.

When I sat by her bed, I would be facing the window, and I would try to point out birds that flew past. Not that there were many. Chimney swifts would circle high in the distance in summer, but they were too far away and too fast for her to see them clearly. Flocks of starlings might sweep past in fall or winter, and those she could see, especially if they were large flocks or if they made repeated passes. But she had never been particularly fond of starlings anyway, so I might tell her that they were blackbirds, or grackles mixed with a few starlings.

Since there was a hospital only a few blocks away to the east, we could hear distant ambulance sirens many times a day, and sometimes a helicopter would arrive, slanting down across the patch of sky that my mother watched. When she heard the beating rotors, she would strain to raise her head a little and watch that chopper coming in. On repeated visits I had noticed, over and over, that she didn't pay that much attention to the departure of the helicopter, even though we could hear the start-up of the rotors and there would have been time to turn and watch it lift off, angle away, on another mission of mercy. No, for some reason, it was the arrival of that big metal bird that seemed to hold meaning for her. I noticed, too, that after each arrival her expression would change. I had the uneasy sense that she could tell, in some supernatural way, what the outcome of the emergency flight was going to be. Her face might take on a more relaxed look, as if she knew that the patient was going to be all right. Or her anxious, pinched expression might suggest a more painful outcome, that the desperate life flight to the hospital had been in vain, arriving too late.

We watched a helicopter come in this afternoon, and afterward her expression was drawn and panicked, and she sank back on the pillow with her eyes wide before turning to look at me again. "Please talk to me," she said. "Please tell me another story."

A Petrel
from Mars

Living in Arizona for so many years, I learned to take water seriously. Water meant more there. Desert people think about water, obsess over it, gravitate to it. We would not respond to water in this way if we lived in a swamp, or at sea. When, as a bird watcher, I protest the other bird watchers' tendency to seek out rare birds and ignore the common ones, I am really railing against a universal fact of human nature, and one that afflicts me just as much, if I'm willing to admit it. We value what is scarce.

But what we were looking at on this particular morning was scarcely a serious body of water. No, in reality this was just a creek, artificially induced to linger and spread out a bit before it slipped through the spillway of the Lake Patagonia Dam and continued trickling toward Nogales. After good rains, the lake could be more than two miles long, but even then it still looked insignificant, overwhelmed by the surrounding dry hills of southern Arizona. On an ordinary day, obviously, no one would come here to seek a bird of the open ocean.

But this was no ordinary day. The remains of a tropical

storm had come powering north across Arizona two nights before, Monday night, with fitful wind and heavy rain, trailing out the last of the fury that it had built up in the warm seas to the south of the Gulf of California. Most tropical storms off the west coast of Mexico travel northwest into the wide Pacific, but the rare one that swings inland may drag a few seabirds with it. Accordingly, I had gone out all day Tuesday to look at all the little ponds lying in the track of the storm.

Those little ponds had produced nothing of novelty, and I had come home convinced that the storm had been a dud. Convinced, until I walked in the door to the sound of a ringing phone. A friend was calling with news from southwestern New Mexico: in the wake of the storm, someone had picked up a strange bird fluttering under a streetlight in Silver City. It was a least storm-petrel — a true oceanic bird, the first member of the seagoing family of storm-petrels ever to be recorded in landlocked New Mexico.

Hanging up the phone, I was thinking, *How odd*. How strange indeed that a storm-petrel should have been carried all the way from the coast of Sonora into New Mexico without even one being put down in the intervening area, in Arizona. Then the phone rang again. It would continue to ring off and on for half the night — because a least storm-petrel *had* been found in Arizona. An out-of-state visitor had found it, quite by chance, late in the afternoon, and had managed to get a local birder out to see it. The storm-petrel had been sitting on the water on Lake Patagonia as the sun went down.

So before the sun came back up again, my friend Will Russell and I were speeding down the highway to the Lake Patagonia turnoff.

Arriving at dawn, we found half a dozen other birders already collected in the parking lot on the south side of the reservoir. Among them was the man who had discovered the storm-petrel the previous day, Peter Kasper, an Australian birder temporarily living in Illinois.

He was a skilled observer, but he had not come to Lake Patagonia for birds. "It was so beastly hot," he told us. "I thought I'd have a swim. Coming back across the lake, I saw this little dark bird on the water — I assumed it was a baby coot. So I thought, I'll see how close I can get. But when I was close, I saw it had an odd little bill. It struck me that it must be a petrel of some kind, and I thought, Arizona is not normal habitat for petrels."

Not normal habitat at all. To confirm this sighting, and perhaps to confirm his own sanity, the man had made frantic calls from a pay phone near the lake. Finally he had connected with Dan Jones in the town of Patagonia. Dan had raced to the lake and joined Kasper. With the last daylight, they had watched through Dan's telescope as the least storm-petrel sat on the water, fluttered about occasionally, and gradually moved westward down the lake. "I thought it looked a bit ill," Kasper remarked. "I don't think it would have flown away overnight."

So where was the bird now? With our telescopes, we scanned those parts of the lake that we could see. Lake Patagonia was several hundred yards wide here, but the water was smooth this morning; we should have been able to see even a small bird like a least storm-petrel some distance away on the glassy surface. But it would have been difficult to make out anything in the shadows of the bank along the far shore, and from our position in the main parking lot, we could see only a small part of the lake. Down the center of the reservoir ran a long, wavering line of floating debris, apparently washed into the lake by rains associated with the tropical storm. If the bird had been sitting quietly among this flotsam, it would have been hard to detect.

For a couple of hours we scoped the water from the few vantage points accessible by road, all within the space of half a mile along the lake's south side. But it was obvious that we were missing a lot of territory. Like any reservoir in hilly country, Lake Patagonia had many narrow arms and coves toward the upper end, and closer to the dam it was too wide for us to examine the far side critically. Some of the birders had to leave to go to work, but Will and I and a couple of others went to the small marina on the lake as soon as it opened. We wanted to see if we could continue our search by taking to the water.

The marina had no motorboats to rent, only rowboats and canoes. Someone suggested that the four of us could rent a rowboat and take turns rowing; but Will, who has lived in Maine and has experience on northern waters, nixed the idea. "Rowboats are heavy and slow," he said. "As soon as you stop rowing, the boat stops moving. We'll cover the lake much more easily if we rent a couple of canoes." So within minutes, Will and I were sitting in a canoe, gliding silently into coves on the north side of the lake, while our friends began their search of the south side.

It had been some time since I'd been in a canoe, but the rhythm of it came back to me quickly. Reach far forward, dig in deeply with the point of the paddle, pull it back in one long and continuous motion. Feather the paddle at the end of the stroke and swing it forward again, barely clearing the water. No splash, no resistance, no wasted effort. Do it right and it's easy as walking. Get in sync with your partner and the canoe will glide ahead, nimble and quick, like a living thing. The body relaxes into the rhythm of the paddle, the eyes scan the surface of the water, the mind is free to follow its own course.

My mind could not avoid this thought: *None of us belongs here.* This canoe is a descendant of the craft that carried tribes of Native Americans across unspoiled lakes and rivers, that carried the French voyageurs on their treks through the Canadian wilderness. Even though this canoe is made of sleek aluminum instead of birch bark or hollowed-out logs, still it is out of place in this desert country. Just as this lake is out of place: no lakes would exist in this region without man-made dams. Just as a seabird like a storm-petrel is seriously out of place here. If I raise my eyes from the water, I see arid hillsides dotted with clumps of cacti, spindly ocotillos, thorny mesquites, typical dry hills of southern Arizona.

Although it was not yet midmorning, the sun was already bearing down with fierce authority. I was wearing a cowboy hat for shade. Will, who had forgotten to bring a hat, had tied a bandanna over his head for protection from the sun; he looked like a pirate. So there they go, the cowboy and the buccaneer, paddling their birch-bark canoe around in the desert to look for seabirds. How far can a metaphor be mixed before it sinks under its own weight? Again I thought: *We are all out of place here.*

This setting was a world away from the usual haunts of storm-petrels. My mind kept filling with images from times I had seen them — never in a place like this, and seldom with my feet on solid ground. To see these birds, and other seabirds, ordinarily we would go to some coastal port city and take a daylong boat trip on the open ocean.

Even where they normally lived, the storm-petrels seemed to not quite belong. The other seabirds were such strong fliers: long-winged albatrosses and shearwaters, masters of the wind, scaling and gliding against the gales, or else muscular power flappers such as skuas. And then there were the little storm-petrels, fluttering along over the surface like black butterflies. They seemed too frail for their formidable surroundings. But that was an illusion: they were completely at home here, far more comfortable here than temporary seafarers like us. We birders might look about at the flat ocean horizon, with no land in sight anywhere, and feel just a trace of unease. Not so the storm-petrels. All their sustenance comes from the sea, and they might go months without seeing land. When the worst storms rage, they simply flutter along in the deep troughs between the waves, securely out of the wind.

Sometimes when we took ocean birding trips, we would lay out a slick of fish oil and other bait to attract birds in close to the boat. Even near at hand, the storm-petrels seemed expressionless — partly because of their flat, dark eyes in dark faces, but also because they appeared to ignore us. Intent on the food on the surface, they seemed oblivious to the boat. Heads down, eyes focused on the water, the storm-petrels would hover above one spot, fly on a few yards, hover for a moment more, settle briefly, then flutter on again. In their simple world of sea and sky, instinct had given them no specific instructions about chugging boats loaded with birders, and they paid no attention to us at all.

At the upper end of the lake, where Sonoita Creek emptied into the reservoir, Will and I met the birders who had been working the coves on the south side. After a brief discussion, we headed down the lake again. This time we followed a zigzag course, angling from the shoreline out to the line of floating debris in the middle of the lake, scanning all the while for any sign of the storm-petrel.

As we paddled, I was remembering a time when friends and I had visited an offshore island where storm-petrels nested. We had arrived in the evening and stayed overnight, knowing that these little seabirds would come and go here only under the protection of darkness.

Long after sunset, after the last light had faded, we began to hear them: a gobbling, cooing, clucking sputter, from here, from there, from all around us, like demons dancing in the air. While we humans stumbled about, our flashlight beams barely penetrating the night mist, the storm-petrels were perfectly at home. Using mysterious senses that we could not even imagine, each bird would be navigating through the blackness to locate the entrance to its nesting burrow. There it would greet its mate and take its place incubating the single egg, while the mate flew out to sea under the cloak of the night.

The following morning, a biologist who worked on the island led us to nesting burrows that he knew were occupied. "Don't worry," he said; "this never makes them desert their nests," and he reached deep into an underground passage to pull out an adult storm-petrel. In his hand, the bird looked even smaller and more fragile than it would have out at sea: barely the size of a robin, a dusky little bird blinking in the sudden light. In its eyes we could detect no sign of fear: nothing but a lack of recognition, a blank and uncomprehending stare. We were totally alien to its world. In this bird's view of life, we could have come from another planet.

Another hour and a half passed as we canoed our way back down the lake. Toward its lower end, the lake was wider, more than a quarter mile in places, and we crossed from one shore to the other several times. We were still scanning for the storm-petrel, but we were beginning to lose hope. Few water birds of any kind were around, aside from a handful of coots. Most of the birds we were detecting were desert species, and we were noting them only by sound, their voices drifting down from the dry hillsides above us. But as we neared the dam, another sound gradually commanded our attention.

For some time now we had been hearing this sound without consciously noticing it, a dull, constant, white noise, like the distant sound of rushing water. Of course: the floodwaters from the storm-driven rain had topped the capacity of the reservoir, and water was pouring over the center of the dam. That was why there was a line of floating sticks and brush and leaves and trash down the center of the lake; that was where the flotsam was going. The sound grew to a muffled roar as we drew closer. Pulling on the paddles to bring the canoe out of the current, we maneuvered cautiously to the far corner of the dam and looked over.

In the steep-sided valley that stretched away below us, the stream was a jumble of leaves, branches, and great logs carried over the dam by the force of the flood. Looking in silence, we knew we were never going to see the least storm-petrel.

At sea, where this bird belonged, water would have made up half of its limited world. It would have known waves and whitecaps and wind-driven spray, currents and tides, and the sometimes unpredictable violence of the sea. But it would have known nothing of this: such a current that quickened from a treacherous flat calm and turned into a sudden cataract in the night, leaping barriers and plunging, in a cascade of debris, to crash onto the rocky streambed at the base of the dam. No, we were never going to see this bird, never even find its crumpled remains. We could only think of the irony that this little petrel, lost in an alien world, clinging to the only element it recognized, should have been betrayed at the end by water.

SHE'S SLEEPING NOW. Mercifully, finally, my mother has taken refuge in sleep.

As always when I come to town, she tries to stay awake as long as she can, not wanting to miss any of this time together, but the effort exhausts her. It's so hard for her to talk, hard even to concentrate and focus on our largely one-sided conversations. By the latter part of the afternoon today, I could see that she was getting drowsy, so I was reading to her more softly, watching as she faded off to sleep, and toward the end I was just reading silently. It would have been hard for me to tell her how the last story ended anyway, so it was better for her to drift into sleep and let her dreams supply a happier ending.

Now she was resting, looking as peaceful as she ever did these days, her face not completely relaxed, her breathing a little ragged. I watched her for a few minutes, thinking of the lives she had lived before her world had become so diminished, and then I left for a while.

I drove down through the center of Wichita and out toward our old neighborhood. I was headed to the house that the family had moved into when we came out west from Indiana, back when I was nine years old. The key to the front door was still on my key ring, and I parked in the deserted driveway and let myself in.

In the living room I stood still for a long minute, looking around.

I know what this is, I said to myself. *This house has become a shrine to foolish false optimism.* Everything is still in place: all the furniture exactly as Mom had it, pictures still on the walls, books still on the bookshelves, magazines still on the coffee table. We're all taking part in the charade: JB stops in every day to make sure the house is okay and to pick up the mail, Ralph comes over and mows the lawn, Carla dusts and vacuums, Rick does any serious maintenance that's needed, and even I stop in when I'm in town to check on things. We're all fooling ourselves, with the best of intentions, as if our positive thinking could affect anything. We're all accomplices in this crime of self-deception, pretending that Mom will get better and come home again. But in our hearts we know that's not going to happen. She's still forcing herself to stay alert and engaged, mostly for us, not for herself, but her body is steadily wasting away. She's never coming home again. Not in this world.

The accumulated relics of an ending life made this place seem even emptier than if there had been nothing in these rooms at all. This had been a home once, filled with warmth and love and laughter, and now it was just a shell, a sad, empty house. I walked through those silent rooms, nothing moving here now except memories, and found myself at the back of the house, standing at the kitchen window. Outside the window was my mother's bird feeder, still pointlessly kept filled. And as I stood looking blankly out the window, two birds flew in together and landed on the feeder.

They were chickadees.

Time stood still for me. I rubbed my eyes, looked again. No doubt about it — two black-capped chickadees, hopping along the edge of the feeder with a jaunty air. Then one took off and the other followed it, flitting up into the big cottonwood that shaded the backyard.

Of course, you idiot, I said to myself. *Of course there are chickadees here. When you and the family moved in here, it was a new housing development without big trees. But that was more than thirty years ago. Now the trees have grown up, and this is a leafy, shady neighborhood. So of course the chickadees have moved in. You were just so sure of yourself, you thought you knew everything, you had your blinders on and missed the obvious. You, you hotshot bird expert, you were wrong, and she was right, and now she's not here to see them.*

I stood there just staring out the window for a long time, and then I walked into the yard. It was evening, and a brilliant sunset was just starting to light up the western sky. My eyes were misted up and I couldn't see very well, but I realized that there were flights of birds going across the sunset, against that burning sky, and I — I couldn't tell what kinds of birds they were. Blinking, trying hard to focus on these flights of big birds, I was suddenly taken by a wild thought, and I said: *Well . . . maybe they're penguins.*

Maybe they are penguins. Maybe they can fly, after all. You've been wrong about so many things — maybe this is one more case where you were wrong and she was right.

Standing there in the yard where I had first stood as a small boy, feeling small again, I was gradually coming to a new realization. I had never understood why my life-long hero, the greatest bird expert of the twentieth century, Roger Tory Peterson, had also been one of the most humble individuals I had ever met. Now it was beginning to make sense. Peterson was enough of an expert to understand that there are no experts — that none of us really knows anything at all compared with the vast universe of things that will remain unknown.

And finally it began to make sense that my mother, who knew so little about bird life, should have settled on favorite birds that were exactly the same ones that had captivated the great ornithologist. Somewhere out there, beyond our ordinary experience, the highest levels of knowledge would converge with the sense of wonder felt by a complete beginner.

My eyes were filling up with tears and I could hardly see at all now, but I had a feeling that out there in the sunset, or just beyond it, flocks of flamingos and penguins must be flying together. And somehow I knew that my mother was flying with them, graceful and free, that she was released from her pain and physical limitations, that she was nineteen again, looking out at a world of infinite possibilities and infinite wonder.